Gospel Light's

ISLAND

CRAFTS FOR KIDS

* Fun at Church,
  Home or School

* Uses Economical,
  Easy-to-Find Supplies

* 46 Fun Craft Projects
  for Children from
  Preschool to Sixth Grade

* Reproducible!

Gospel Light

HOW TO MAKE CLEAN COPIES FROM THIS BOOK

You may make copies of portions of this book with a clean conscience if

◆ you (or someone in your organization) are the original purchaser;

◆ you are using the copies you make for a noncommercial purpose (such as teaching or promoting your ministry) within your church or organization;

◆ you follow the instructions provided in this book.

However, it is ILLEGAL for you to make copies if

◆ you are using the material to promote, advertise or sell a product or service other than for ministry fund-raising;

◆ you are using the material in or on a product for sale; or

◆ you or your organization are not the original purchaser of this book.

By following these guidelines you help us keep our products affordable.

Thank you,
Gospel Light

GOSPEL LIGHT VACATION BIBLE SCHOOL

Senior Managing Editor, Sheryl Haystead ◆ **Senior Editor,** Heather Kempton ◆ **Assistant Editor,** Becky Garcia ◆ **Contributing Editors,** Suzanne Bass, Deborah Barber, Carol Eide, Cindy Ethier, Kim Fiano, Karen McGraw, Dianne Rowell ◆ **Art Directors,** Lori Hamilton, Samantha Hsu, Lenndy McCullough ◆ **Senior Designer,** Carolyn Thomas

Founder, Dr. Henrietta Mears ◆ **Publisher,** William T. Greig ◆ **Senior Consulting Publisher,** Dr. Elmer L. Towns ◆ **Senior Consulting Editor,** Wesley Haystead, M.S.Ed. ◆ **Senior Editor, Biblical and Theological Issues,** Bayard Taylor, M.Div.

Contents

introduction

Island Fun!

A tropical island brings to mind bright colorful flowers, swaying palm trees and warm, breezy afternoons at the beach. Children love the textures, sights and smells of the ocean. The fun of exploring a tropical beach is the inspiration behind the crafts of this resource book, *Island Crafts for Kids*. Your students will have oceans of fun as they create these colorful crafts.

In addition to learning about sea and island life, your students will also daily explore God's love for them and what it means to show His love to others. As the children create their crafts together, look for times when they demonstrate patience and kindness. Remind them that love is shown through our actions. Many of these crafts focus on the demonstration of love and kindness in your students' lives, as well as the lives of various people from the Bible.

We hope that you and your students will enjoy many fun-filled hours creating these projects from *Island Crafts for Kids*.

Personalize It!

Feel free to alter the craft materials and instructions in this book to suit your children's needs. Consider what materials you have on hand, what materials are available in your area and what materials you can afford to purchase. In some cases, you may be able to substitute materials you already have for the suggested craft supplies.

In addition, don't feel confined to the crafts in a particular age-level section. You may want to adapt a craft for younger or older children by using the simplification or enrichment ideas where provided.

Three Keys to Success

How can you make craft time successful and fun for your children? First, encourage creativity in each child! Remember, the process of creating is more important than the final product. Provide a variety of materials with which children may work. Allow children to make choices on their own. Don't insist that children "stay inside the lines."

Second, choose projects that are appropriate for the skill level of your children. Children can become discouraged when a project is too difficult for them. Finding the right projects for your children will increase the likelihood that they will be successful and satisfied with their finished products.

Finally, show an interest in the unique way each child approaches a project. Affirm the choices he or she has made. Treat each child's final product as a masterpiece!

The comments you give a child today can affect the way he or she views art in the future, so be positive! Being creative is part of being made in the image of God, the ultimate creator!

Craft Symbols

Some of the craft projects in *Island Crafts for Kids* are appropriate for more than one age level. Next to the title of certain projects, you'll find the symbol shown below. This symbol tells which projects are suitable or adaptable for all elementary-age children—first through sixth grades. As you select projects, consider the particular children you are working with. Feel free to use your own ideas to make projects simpler or more challenging, depending on the needs of your children.

In addition, some craft projects in this book require less preparation than others. The symbol shown below tells which projects require minimal preparation.

suitable for all ages

minimal preparation

Be Prepared

If you are planning to use crafts with a child at home, here are some helpful tips:

◇ Focus on crafts designed for your child's age, but don't ignore projects for older or younger ages. Elementary-age children enjoy many of the projects geared for preschool and kindergarten children. And younger children are always interested in doing "big kid" things. Just plan on working along with your child, helping with tasks he or she can't handle alone.

◇ Start with projects that call for materials you have around the house. Make a list of items you do not have, and plan to gather them in one expedition.

◇ If certain materials seem too difficult to obtain, a little thought can usually lead to appropriate substitutions. Often your creative twist ends up being an improvement over the original plan.

If you are planning to lead a group of children in doing craft projects, keep these hints in mind:

◇ Choose projects that allow children to work with a variety of materials.

◇ Make your project selections far enough in advance to allow time to gather all needed supplies.

◇ Make a sample of each project to be sure the directions are fully understood and that potential problems can be avoided. **You may want to adapt some projects by simplifying procedures or varying the materials.**

◇ Items can often be acquired as donations from people or businesses if you plan ahead and make your needs known. Many churches distribute lists of needed materials to their congregations. Some items can be brought by the children themselves.

◇ In making your supply list, distinguish between items that each individual child will need and those that will be shared among a group.

◇ Keep in mind that some materials may be shared among more than one age level. To avoid frustration, coordinate with other groups that might be using the same supplies you need so that children can complete their craft projects. Basic supplies that are used in many projects, such as glue, scissors, markers, etc., should be available in every craft room.

Crafts with a Message

Many projects in *Island Crafts for Kids* can easily become crafts with a message. Have children create slogans or poetry as part of their projects; or provide photocopies of an appropriate poem, thought or Bible verse for children to attach to their crafts. Below are some examples of ways to use messages to enhance the craft projects in this book.

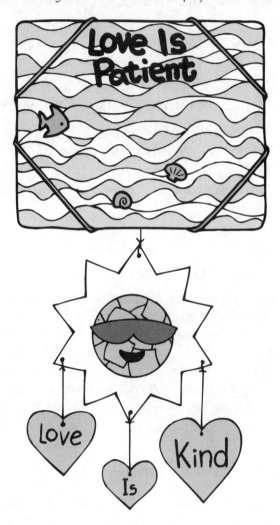

Treasure Talk

Each craft in this book includes Treasure Talk, a section designed to help you enhance craft times with thought-provoking conversation that is age appropriate. The Treasure Talk for a project may relate to prayer, a Scripture verse or a Bible story. Often Treasure Talk includes interesting facts about marine animals. If your craft program includes large groups of children, share these conversation suggestions with each helper, who can use them with individuals or small groups.

Helpful Hints

Using Glue with Young Children

Since preschoolers have difficulty using glue bottles effectively, you may want to try one of the following procedures. Purchase glue in large containers (up to one gallon size).

a. Pour small amounts of glue into several margarine tubs.

b. Dilute glue by mixing a little water into each container.

c. Children use paintbrushes to spread glue on their projects.

d. When project is completed, place lids on margarine tubs to save glue for future projects.

OR

a. Pour small amounts of glue into several margarine tubs.

b. Give each child a cotton swab.

c. Children dip cotton swabs into the glue and rub glue on projects.

d. When project is completed, place lids on margarine tubs to save glue for future projects.

glue level   swabs

Cutting with Scissors

When cutting with scissors is required for crafts, remember that some children in your class may be left-handed. It is very difficult for a left-handed person to cut with right-handed scissors. Have available two or three pairs of left-handed scissors. These can be obtained from a school supply center.

If your craft involves cutting fabric, felt or ribbon, have available several pairs of fabric scissors for older children.

Using Acrylic Paints

Acrylic paints are required for several projects. Our suggestions:

◆ Provide smocks or old shirts for your children to wear, as acrylics may stain clothes.

◆ Acrylics can be expensive for a large group of children. To make paint go further, dilute it with a small amount of water. Or use house paints thinned with water.

◆ Fill shallow containers with soapy water. Clean paintbrushes before switching colors and immediately after finishing project.

Leading a Child to Christ

One of the greatest privileges of serving in VBS is helping children become members of God's family. Pray for the children you teach and ask God to prepare them to understand and receive the good news about Jesus. Ask God to give you the sensitivity and wisdom you need to communicate effectively and to be aware of opportunities that occur naturally.

Because children are easily influenced to follow the group, be cautious about asking for group decisions. Offer opportunities to talk and pray individually with any child who expresses interest in becoming a member of God's family—but without pressure. A good way to guard against coercing a child to respond is to simply ask, "Would you like to hear more about this now or at another time?"

When talking about salvation with children, use words and phrases they understand; never assume they understand a concept just because they can repeat certain words. Avoid symbolic terms ("born again," "ask Jesus to come into your heart," "open your heart," etc.) that will confuse these literal-minded thinkers. (You may also use the evangelism booklet *God Loves You!*)

1. God wants you to become His child. Why do you think He wants you in His family? (See 1 John 3:1.)

2. Every person in the world has done wrong things. The Bible word for doing wrong is "sin." What do you think should happen to us when we sin? (See Romans 6:23.)

3. God loves you so much that He sent His Son to die on the cross to take the punishment for your sin. Because Jesus never sinned, He is the only One who can take the punishment for your sin. (See 1 Corinthians 15:3; 1 John 4:14.)

4. Are you sorry for your sin? Tell God that you are. Do you believe Jesus died for your sin and then rose again? Tell Him that, too. If you tell God you are sorry for your sin and believe that Jesus died to take your sin away, God forgives you. (See 1 John 1:9.)

5. The Bible says that when you believe Jesus is God's Son and is alive today, you receive God's gift of eternal life. This gift makes you a child of God. (See John 3:16.) This means God is with you now and forever.

There is great value in encouraging a child to think and pray about what you have said before responding. Encourage the child who makes a decision to become a Christian to tell his or her parents. Give your pastor and the child's Sunday School teacher(s) his or her name. A child's initial response to Jesus is just the beginning of a lifelong process of growing in the faith, so children who make decisions need to be followed up to help them grow. The discipling booklet *Growing as God's Child* is an effective tool to use.

Age-Level Characteristics Ages 4 and 5

SonTreasure Island prekindergarten and kindergarten materials have been planned for children who are three to six years old with a ratio of one teacher for every four to six children (and can be easily adapted to include two-year-olds with a ratio of one teacher for every four children). Each activity provides enough flexibility so that young children can work successfully. Effectively instructing children of varying ages requires a teacher to recognize and accept wide individual differences in skills, abilities and interests. Regardless of the level at which a child works, a teacher can use the child's interest in the activity to guide his or her thinking toward understanding a Bible truth.

Bible Learning Activities

THREE- and FOUR-YEAR-OLDS need free play and careful supervision. They often pursue different activities, having little interest in cooperative play. Provide books and puzzles for children who are not interested in the activities offered, but engage children in conversation related to the day's lesson as they work. KINDERGARTNERS enjoy experimenting with a variety of materials and tools. Their verbal skills and enjoyment of other children make play more purposeful and interactive.

THREES and FOURS use blocks in an exploratory manner, stacking and moving them in a seemingly random fashion. Occasionally extend children's play by offer-

ing specific building instructions as suggested in the lesson. KINDERGARTNERS usually plan what they will build and then use the construction to play out an imaginary event. They incorporate accessories such as toy cars and animals in the building.

THREES and FOURS are just beginning to use art supplies and often find the finished product of little interest. Encourage them to try new things, but don't expect beauty or design. KINDERGARTNERS enjoy exploring the use of art materials but may find the process tedious after a short while. To sustain their interest, offer encouragement and assistance as needed.

Large-Group Times

THREES AND FOURS need a variety of brief activities during a large-group experience. Puppets provide visual interest, but keep puppet dialogue to a minimum. Because children do not have a backlog of experiences to help them recall an idea or object, show pictures and objects to illustrate conversation and activities.

KINDERGARTNERS enjoy talking about things they have seen and done and will enjoy interacting with puppets. When the conversation relates to a common experience, most children are interested in hearing other children recount events. Avoid letting any one child dominate the conversation.

Because repetition is essential to a child's learning process, he or she needs to hear and sing the same songs again and again. Repeat familiar songs for THREES and FOURS. Introduce more of the songs suggested in each lesson for KINDERGARTNERS.

Bible Story/Application

To accommodate the attention span of THREES and FOURS, keep the Bible story very brief. Illustrate story action with visuals from *Prekindergarten/Kindergarten Teaching Resources*. Ask simple questions to help children recall Bible facts that are obvious in the story and visuals.

Even though KINDERGARTNERS have a slightly longer attention span, tell the Bible stories without elaboration. They enjoy the challenge of what-do-you-think questions.

Age-Level Characteristics Grades 1 and 2

Physical

The term "perpetual motion" may be used to describe children this age. Small-muscle coordination is still developing and improving. Girls are ahead of boys at this stage of development.

Teaching Tip: Give children opportunities for movement during every class session.

Social

Children are concerned with pleasing their leaders. Each child is also struggling to become socially acceptable to the peer group. The Golden Rule is a tough concept at this age. Being first and winning are very important. Taking turns is hard, but this skill improves by the end of the second grade. A child's social process moves gradually from *I* to *you* and *we*.

Teaching Tips: Provide opportunities for children to practice taking turns. Help each child accept the opinions and wishes of others and consider the welfare of the group as well as his or her own welfare. Call attention to times when the group cooperated successfully.

Spiritual

Children can sense the greatness, wonder and love of God when helped with visual and specific examples. The nonphysical nature of God is baffling, but God's presence in every area of life is generally accepted when parents and teachers communicate this belief by their attitudes and actions. Children can think of Jesus as a friend, but they need specific examples of how Jesus expresses love and care. This understanding leads many children to belief and acceptance of Jesus as personal Savior. Children can comprehend talking to God anywhere, anytime and in their own words; and they need regular opportunities to pray.

Teaching Tip: The gospel becomes real as children feel love from those who talk about God. Show your faith in a consistent, loving way to model the loving nature of God to children.

Emotional

Children are experiencing new and frequently intense feelings as they grow in independence. Sometimes the child finds it hard to control his or her behavior. There is still a deep need for approval from adults and a growing need for approval by peers.

Teaching Tips: Seek opportunities to help each child in your group KNOW and FEEL you love him or her. Show genuine interest in each child and his or her activities and accomplishments. Learn children's names and use them frequently in positive ways.

Cognitive

There is an intense eagerness to learn, and children of this age ask lots of questions. They like to repeat stories and activities. The concept of time is limited. Thinking is here and now, rather than past or future. Listening and speaking skills are developing rapidly; girls are ahead of boys. Each child thinks everyone shares his or her view. Children see parts, rather than how the parts make up the whole, and they think very literally.

Teaching Tip: Talk simply and clearly, avoiding words the child may not understand.

Age-Level Characteristics Grades 3 and 4

Physical

Children at this level have good large- and small-muscle coordination. The girls are generally ahead of the boys. Children can work diligently for longer periods but can become impatient with delays or their own imperfect abilities.

Teaching Tip: The two Set the Story activities in each lesson provide options for including physical activity in this center.

Social

Children's desire for status within the peer group becomes more intense. Most children remain shy with strangers and exhibit strong preferences for being with a few close friends. Some children still lack essential social skills needed to make and retain friendships.

Teaching Tip: Look for the child who needs a friend. Sit next to that child and include him or her in what you are doing.

Spiritual

Children are open to sensing the need for God's continuous help and guidance. They can recognize the need for a personal Savior. There may be a desire to become a member of God's family. Children who indicate an awareness of sin and a concern about accepting Jesus as Savior need careful guidance without pressure.

Teaching Tips: Give children opportunities to pray. Talk about the forgiving nature of God. Talk personally with a child who shows interest in trusting the Lord Jesus. Use the *God Loves You!* booklet to explain how to become a Christian.

Emotional

This is the age of teasing, nicknames, criticism and increased verbal skills to vent anger. By eight years of age, children have developed a sense of fair play and a value system of right and wrong. At nine years of age, children are searching for identity beyond membership in the family unit.

Teaching Tips: You have a great opportunity to be a Christian example at a time when children are eagerly searching for models! Encourage children's creativity and boost their self-concept. Let children know by your words and by your actions that "love is spoken here" and that you will not let others hurt them or let them hurt others.

Cognitive

Children are beginning to realize there may be valid opinions besides their own. They are becoming able to evaluate alternatives and are less likely than before to fasten onto one viewpoint as the only one possible. Children are also beginning to think in terms of "the whole." Children think more conceptually and have a high level of creativity. By this stage, however, many children have become self-conscious as their understanding has grown to exceed their abilities in some areas.

Teaching Tips: Encourage children to use their Bibles by finding and reading portions of Scripture. Help children understand the meaning of the verses they memorize.

Age-Level Characteristics Grades 5 and 6

Physical

Children have mastered most basic physical skills, are active and curious, and seek a variety of new experiences. Rapid growth can cause some 11-year-olds to tire easily.

Teaching Tip: Provide children with a balance of same-gender and mixed-gender activities.

Social

Friendships and activities with their peers flourish. Children draw together and away from adults in the desire for independence. The child wants to be a part of a same-gender group and usually does not want to stand alone in competition.

Teaching Tip: Listen, ask questions and avoid being judgmental.

Spiritual

Children can have deep feelings of love for God, can share the good news of Jesus with a friend and are capable of involvement in outreach and service projects. The child may seek guidance from God to make everyday and long-range decisions.

Teaching Tips: Provide opportunities for children to make choices and decisions based on Bible concepts. Involve children in work and service projects.

Emotional

Children are usually cooperative, easygoing, content, friendly and agreeable. Be aware that often 11-year-old children are experiencing unsteady emotions and can quickly shift from one mood to another.

Teaching Tips: Be patient with changes of feelings. Give many opportunities to make choices with only a few necessary limits. Take time to listen as students share their experiences and problems with you.

Cognitive

Children of this age are verbal! Making ethical decisions becomes a challenging task. They are able to express ideas and feelings in a creative way. By 11 years old, children have begun to be able to reason abstractly. They begin to think of themselves as grown up and at the same time question adult concepts. Hero worship is strong.

Teaching Tips: Include lots of opportunities for talking, questioning and discussing in a safe, accepting environment. Ask children for their ideas of how things could be done better.

Decorating Your Craft Center

Dragonfly Falls

Create a tall waterfall in your craft center. Cut a piece of sturdy cardboard 8 inches (20.5 cm) deep and as wide as you want your waterfall to be. Measure 2 inches (5 cm) on one long side of the cardboard, score with a craft knife and bend (sketch a). Glue lengths of blue crepe paper streamers, Mylar and satin gift-wrap ribbon or strips of transparent blue cellophane to the opposite edge of the board. Tack the scored edge to a wall to mount the waterfall.

Create a pool and stream flowing from the waterfall. Cut blue butcher paper to form a small pool and stream, or lay blue fabric on the floor. To create a transparent look, add a layer of clear or blue cellophane, plastic food wrap, clear vinyl sheeting or a plastic shower curtain. Between the two layers place some pebbles, toy fish and frogs, and scatter sequins to look like sparkling bubbles. Pull fiberfill stuffing apart to form wispy pieces and place at the base of the falls to look like foam. Set rocks along the edges of the pool or stream and add large plastic frogs.

Crumple brown or black paper and tape to the wall to look like the rocky face of a cliff surrounding the waterfall.

Use hot glue to glue pockets of sphagnum moss, artificial greenery and flowers to spots on the rock wall.

Enlarge the Volcano Island pattern found in *Reproducible Resources* on butcher paper, paint and attach to one wall. Set out potted plants or create Paper Palms and Plants following instructions in *Reproducible Resources*.

Make several giant dragonflies using the dragonfly pattern from *Reproducible Resources*. Paint the body in bright or iridescent colors and hang from the ceiling. Make smaller dragonflies to hover over the pond and stream. (Use the instructions for Clothespin Dragonflies found on p. 49.) Cut large lily pads out of green craft foam. Poke a wire through each lily pad, and stick a piece of clay on the end of the wire under the lily pad to make it stand. Attach the other end of the wire to a Clothespin Dragonfly (sketch b). Set the lily pad on the pond, with the dragonfly hovering above it on the wire.

a. Bend cardboard. streamers

b. craft foam lily pad clay

SonTreasure Island VBS Craft Leader's Guide

If you'll be leading crafts at SonTreasure Island Vacation Bible School, *Island Crafts for Kids* contains more than enough crafts for each age level. For additional hints about leading a group of children in craft projects, see "Be Prepared" on page 5.

The projects in this book can be done in individual classrooms or in a Craft Center. Here's how a Craft Center works:

◈ Select projects that will appeal to several age levels. (Sometimes you'll find one project that all children will enjoy making. Other times you'll need to select one project for the younger children and one for the older children.)

◈ Recruit adults and/or youths to prepare for and run the Craft Center.

◈ Decorate your center with samples of crafts your kids will be making.

◈ As classes visit the Craft Center, lead them in making projects, tailoring instructions and conversation to the children's age level.

The Craft Coordinator—A Very Important Person

As Craft Coordinator, you play a key role in determining the quality of your craft program. Here are four crucial steps in achieving success at your task:

1. Plan ahead. Familiarize yourself with each day's craft project and plan any necessary changes.
2. Be well organized (see "SonTreasure Island Countdown Schedule").
3. Secure your supplies in advance. Prepare a bulletin notice listing items you need donated from members of your congregation. Also, people are often happy to help if you personally ask them to donate or purchase specific items.
4. Communicate with everyone involved. People who do not know what to do may not ask for help.

SonTreasure Island Countdown Schedule

16 weeks before:
1. List all staff needs. (Determine if crafts will be led by regular teachers or by special craft leaders and if students from the Youth Department will serve as craft helpers.)
2. Meet with the VBS Director to compile a list of prospective staff.
3. Begin personal contacts to recruit needed staff.

12 weeks before:
1. Select projects from this book and list needed supplies.
2. Determine which items are already on hand and which need to be secured.

8 weeks before:
1. Distribute a bulletin notice listing needed supplies.
2. Begin organizing supplies as they are acquired. Separate inventories for each age group are often helpful, especially in large programs.

6 weeks before:
1. Review staffing needs with the VBS Director and plan involvement in training session.
2. Assign leaders to make a sample of each craft project that they will teach to children.
3. Distribute second notice regarding supplies.

4 weeks before:
1. Participate in training session, showing samples of at least the first-day craft projects.
2. Distribute third notice regarding supplies.
3. Make any needed personal contacts to gather required supplies.

2 weeks before:
1. Purchase any supplies still needed. Adjust supplies as needed.

During VBS:
1. Make sure needed supplies are available for staff.
2. Secure additional supplies as needed.

SonTreasure Island Course Description

Who wouldn't want to explore a Caribbean island, with its glittering turquoise waters, warm white sands and cool ocean breezes? Visitors to SonTreasure Island are welcomed by the scent of exotic flowers, the taste of tropical fruits and the captivating sound of a steel-drum band. But this is no ordinary tropical escape! There is treasure to be found here. More precious than gold, more lasting than diamonds, it is the greatest treasure of all—God's love!

The Christian life begins with God's love for us and continues as His love flows through us to others. At SonTreasure Island, your treasure seekers will play island games, create colorful crafts and enjoy tropical snacks. But more important, they will discover the rich treasure of God's love through the truths found in 1 Corinthians 13.

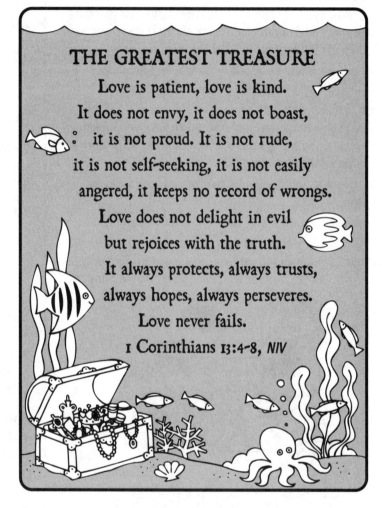

THE GREATEST TREASURE

Love is patient, love is kind. It does not envy, it does not boast, it is not proud. It is not rude, it is not self-seeking, it is not easily angered, it keeps no record of wrongs. Love does not delight in evil but rejoices with the truth. It always protects, always trusts, always hopes, always perseveres. Love never fails.

1 Corinthians 13:4-8, *NIV*

Each day your children will learn how Jesus' life illustrates one of five key truths about God's love as described in this treasured passage of Scripture. They'll learn that because **God's Love Is Giving**, He sent His only Son, Jesus, to show His love to us. They will learn that Jesus helped a young girl and a sick woman because **God's Love Is Kind**. Through Jesus' compassion for a Samaritan woman, they will learn that **God's Love Is Caring**. Jesus' friendship with the tax collector Zacchaeus will show them that **God's Love Is Forgiving**. Finally, your children will discover that through Jesus' death and resurrection, we can know that **God's Love Is Forever**.

SonTreasure Island Course Overview and Suggested Crafts

Below is an overview of SonTreasure Island VBS with suggested projects for each age level. Each craft has been selected to reinforce the Bible story, lesson focus or memory verse of the day. All projects are fully described in this book.

Session	Bible Story	Focus	Bible Memory Verse	Suggested Crafts
1	**God Gives Us Jesus** Matthew 1:18-25; 3; 4:23-25; Luke 1:11-60; 2:1-20	God's love is shown in Jesus.	**Early Childhood** God loved us: He sent His Son. (See 1 John 4:9.) **Elementary** "This is how God showed his love among us: He sent his one and only Son into the world that we might live through him." 1 John 4:9	**Early Childhood** Nativity Scene Diorama **Primary** Nativity Bag **Middler** Scented Seascape Jar **Preteen** Nativity Box
2	**Jesus Helps a Young Girl and a Sick Woman** Matthew 9:18-26; Mark 5:21-43; Luke 8:40-56	God's love is kind and patient.	**Early Childhood** Love is patient, love is kind. 1 Corinthians 13:4 **Elementary** "Love is patient, love is kind. It does not envy, it does not boast, it is not proud." 1 Corinthians 13:4	**Early Childhood** Love Is Kind Mobile **Primary** Underwater Verse **Middler** Fishbowl Tic-Tac-Toe **Preteen** Oil Drum Painting
3	**Jesus Cares for a Samaritan Woman** John 4:1-42	God's love is for everyone.	**Early Childhood** [Love] is not rude. 1 Corinthians 13:5 **Elementary** "[Love] is not rude, it is not self-seeking." 1 Corinthians 13:5	**Early Childhood** Woman at the Well **Primary** Precious Jewels Treasure Chest **Middler** Clothespin Dragonfly **Preteen** Ocean Wind Chime
4	**Jesus Forgives Zacchaeus** Luke 19:1-10	God's love is forgiving.	**Early Childhood** [Love] is not easily angered. 1 Corinthians 13:5 **Elementary** "[Love] is not easily angered, it keeps no record of wrongs. Love does not delight in evil but rejoices with the truth." 1 Corinthians 13:5-6	**Early Childhood** Zacchaeus Puppet Theater **Primary** Zacchaeus, You Come Down! **Middler** Island Maracas **Preteen** I Want to See Jesus Maze
5	**Jesus Lives Forever** Mark 14:27—16:20; Luke 22:47—24:53; John 21:15-17	God's love never fails.	**Early Childhood** Love lasts forever. (See 1 Corinthians 13:7.) **Elementary** "[Love] always protects, always trusts, always hopes, always perseveres. Love never fails." 1 Corinthians 13:7-8	**Early Childhood** Good News Treasure Carriers **Primary** Pop-Up Easter Card **Middler** SonTreasure Island Visor **Preteen** Forever Sandcastles

Session One
God Gives Us Jesus

Scripture

Matthew 1:18-25; 3; 4:23-25;
Luke 1:11-60; 2:1-20

Bible Memory Verse

This is how God showed his love among us: He sent his one and only Son into the world that we might live through him.
1 John 4:9

Lesson Focus

God's love is shown in Jesus.

Bible Aims

During this session, each student may
1. DISCOVER that God sent His Son, Jesus, to show His love for us;
2. DESCRIBE situations in which to show God's love to others;
3. ASK God for help to show His love to others;
4. PRAY to become a member of God's family, as the Holy Spirit leads.

Bible Story Recap

One day an angel told Zechariah and his wife, Elizabeth, that they would have a son named John. John would help people prepare for the promised Savior. Angels then visited Elizabeth's cousin Mary and Joseph, the man Mary was engaged to marry. The angels said that Mary would have God's Son—the Savior! Mary's baby was born in Bethlehem and named Jesus.

After the babies grew up, Jesus went to the Jordan River. John was baptizing people who wanted forgiveness for their sins. Jesus asked John to baptize Him. John knew Jesus hadn't done anything wrong. He thought Jesus should baptize him instead! But Jesus obeyed God in everything and insisted John baptize Him. After the baptism, a voice from heaven said, "This is my Son, whom I love; with him I am well pleased" (Matthew 3:17). God sent His Son, Jesus, to show His love for us.

Teacher's Devotional

"Nothin' says lovin' like somethin' from the oven!" Or at least that's what an old advertising jingle would have you believe. But the advertiser was selling a prepared product and implying that your family would never notice the difference between it and something made from scratch. A baked expression of love could be easy and convenient or it could be difficult and inconvenient, involving time and fresh ingredients! The advertiser would have us believe that the effort required by both methods was the same.

As you might suspect, what people think about love can be a lot like that advertiser's message: Love should be easy and convenient. It should just happen, like a chemical reaction. But what is God's definition of love? First John 3:16 tells us, "This is how we know what love is: Jesus Christ laid down his life for us." When Jesus surrendered His life for us, He did not do what was easy or convenient. Jesus showed us *agape* love—total and complete.

Before your week of VBS work begins, take time to consider your definition of love. How closely does it align with Jesus' definition? Then commit yourself to do cheerfully the work that will be needed—whether easy or difficult, convenient or inconvenient. Ask God to help you show His love, especially during trying moments. God has put you in this place, this week, to help children learn to know what His love really is!

Jesus Helps a Young Girl and a Sick Woman

Scripture

Matthew 9:18-26; Mark 5:21-43; Luke 8:40-56

Bible Memory Verse

Love is patient, love is kind. It does not envy, it does not boast, it is not proud. 1 Corinthians 13:4

Lesson Focus

God's love is kind and patient.

Bible Aims

During this session, each student may

1. DISCOVER that Jesus showed God's love by healing a young girl and a sick woman;
2. IDENTIFY kind and patient actions that show concern for others and their problems;
3. ASK God to help him or her show kind and patient actions in specific situations;
4. PRAY to become a member of God's family, as the Holy Spirit leads.

Bible Story Recap

A large crowd gathered to see Jesus. Jairus pushed his way through the crowd and asked Jesus for help. Jairus's daughter was very sick. Jesus agreed to help, and they began walking toward Jairus's house. Then Jesus felt something. Someone had grabbed His robe! When Jesus asked who had touched Him, a woman fearfully came forward. She told Jesus that she had been sick for 12 years, but she knew if she could just touch Him, she'd be made well. Again, Jesus was loving and kind and healed the woman.

As they neared Jairus's house, several men told them Jairus's daughter had already died. Jesus told Jairus to believe and kept walking to the house. The little girl was lying in her bed. Jesus told her to get up, and she did! Everyone was amazed and happy. Jesus showed God's love by healing a young girl and a sick woman.

Teacher's Devotional

Late-afternoon checkout lines at grocery stores can reveal a lot about human character. Amid beeping machines and wailing toddlers, you might hear "That doesn't look like fewer than 10 items!" or "Why do I always get behind someone with coupons?" or "Why doesn't she make that child hush?" Even if we consider ourselves too kind to actually say such things aloud, we often think them, or maybe we throw a dirty look or two—filled with rising irritation at the thoughtlessness of others!

In contrast, love in action is patient and kind. It behaves with humility and doesn't focus exclusively on personal agendas or achievements. Love expressed through patience is not so much about waiting as about being fully present where we are, in the present moment. Living expectantly in the here and now reminds us that God has placed us in situations He has designed for us. Ephesians 2:10 tells us, "For we are God's workmanship, created in Christ Jesus to do good works, which God prepared in advance for us to do."

Trusting God's design for every moment of our lives means that we can practice love in every difficult situation. We can pray for those who tax our patience, trusting that God's love and kindness can prevail in every circumstance. As you work with God's children this week, find ways to share the treasure of God's love, even in the most difficult moments.

Session Three

Jesus Cares for a Samaritan Woman

Scripture

John 4:1-42

Bible Memory Verse

[Love] is not rude, it is not self-seeking.
1 Corinthians 13:5

Lesson Focus

God's love is for everyone.

Bible Aims

During this session, each student may
1. DISCOVER that Jesus showed God's love to a Samaritan woman whom others might have ignored;
2. IDENTIFY situations in which it might be hard to show God's love;
3. ASK God to help him or her show God's love to people whom others may not care about;
4. PRAY to become a member of God's family, as the Holy Spirit leads.

Bible Story Recap

One day Jesus and His friends were in Samaria. They came to a well and Jesus sat down to rest. His friends went to the nearby town to buy food. Then a woman came to get water at the well. Jesus asked her for a drink of water. The woman was surprised! Men rarely spoke to women, and Jews almost NEVER spoke to Samaritans! Jesus showed God's love to a woman most people would have expected Him to ignore.

Jesus and the woman talked and Jesus told her He could give her living water. Jesus meant He could give her life from God that would last forever. Jesus told her so many amazing things that the woman ran to the town and told everyone about Jesus, the Savior! Many people believed that Jesus was the Savior.

Teacher's Devotional

The car that just cut you off has a bumper sticker that reads, "It's all about ME!" More than ever, people seem to accept rude, selfish behavior as acceptable, perhaps even desirable. The current thinking seems to hold that it's okay to show love to others, but the most important thing is to love yourself first.

What does authentic love, God's love, teach us about dealing with others? Considering another person first—regardless of power, popularity or position—expresses love free from rudeness and self-seeking. God's love for us is the only real basis for our personal dignity or worth. Contrast Jesus' words to the outcast, derided Samaritan woman with the ways pagan cultures treat their weak, poor or outcast. Only God's love and grace give us the ability to show others kind behavior, gracious words and unselfish deeds.

Compassion and consideration for others is a natural outgrowth of receiving God's unconditional love in Christ. Only forgiven hearts produce genuinely loving actions and attitudes. When we show grace to another, instead of being rude or self-seeking, our actions acknowledge that we have received God's grace. It also gives both example and permission to the forgiven one to show grace to another. A worldwide revolution in true love begins right here, right now—as we show God's love to the children in our classes, our VBS coworkers and the other people we encounter in our everyday lives.

Jesus Forgives Zacchaeus

Scripture

Luke 19:1-10

Bible Memory Verse

[Love] is not easily angered, it keeps no record of wrongs. Love does not delight in evil but rejoices with the truth.
1 Corinthians 13:5-6

Lesson Focus

God's love is forgiving.

Bible Aims

During this session, each student may
1. DISCOVER that Jesus showed God's love by forgiving Zacchaeus, the tax collector;
2. DESCRIBE actions that show forgiveness to others;
3. ASK God to help him or her forgive others;
4. PRAY to become a member of God's family, as the Holy Spirit leads.

Bible Story Recap

When Jesus and His friends went to Jericho, people lined the streets just to see Jesus. One man, a tax collector named Zacchaeus, was too short to see over the people around him. He wanted to see Jesus so much that he climbed up a tree. Then Jesus surprised Zacchaeus. Jesus walked right up to the tree and told Zacchaeus to come down. Jesus wanted to have dinner at Zacchaeus's house!

Everyone was surprised that Jesus would be kind to a sinner like Zacchaeus. Tax collectors were known as cheats and thieves! But Jesus' kindness and love changed Zacchaeus. Zacchaeus said that he would give back FOUR times the money he'd taken unfairly and HALF of all he had to the poor. Jesus forgave Zacchaeus for the wrong things he'd done.

Teacher's Devotional

Some of us are planners. We neatly file all records, regularly balance the books and use spreadsheets to calculate our debts and assets. Zacchaeus, the tax collector, was probably a planner. Judging by his wealth and his neighbors' dislike of him, he was probably very thorough. He may have even kept a neat set of DOUBLE books—one for the Romans and one for himself.

Planners probably also understand Zacchaeus's initial shock when Jesus called him down from the tree and invited Himself to dinner. That appointment was not in Zacchaeus's personal planner—not even in pencil! But in one act and one statement, Jesus lavished Zacchaeus with a love, forgiveness and acceptance that Zacchaeus had never known. It didn't take Zacchaeus long to recover his balance. He realized the great grace he'd received and declared that he was giving back four-fold to anyone he'd cheated!

Whether or not we balance our books and file our receipts, there is one area of accounting in which we can relax: We need never keep any record of wrong! Jesus tells us to stop keeping our own double sets of books—our "Christian" set and another set in which we note in permanent ink unpaid debts. As forgiven followers of Jesus, we are free to forgive all debts, burn the old records and let Him free us from the pain, bitterness and frustration bound up in every one of those old accounts. The forgiveness God lavishes in Jesus' name frees you to focus on giving your students the greatest treasure ever—God's amazing love!

Jesus Lives Forever

Scripture

Mark 14:27—16:20; Luke 22:47—24:53; John 21:15-17

Bible Memory Verse

[Love] always protects, always trusts, always hopes, always perseveres. Love never fails. 1 Corinthians 13:7-8

Lesson Focus

God's love never fails.

Bible Aims

During this session, each student may
1. DISCOVER that Jesus died and rose again so that we can experience God's love and be in His family forever;
2. DESCRIBE situations in which it helps to remember God's love;
3. THANK God for offering him or her God's eternal love through His Son, Jesus;
4. PRAY to become a member of God's family, as the Holy Spirit leads.

Bible Story Recap

One night Jesus and His friends went to a garden to pray. Suddenly, soldiers appeared and arrested Jesus! Peter was so angry, he cut off a soldier's ear. Jesus told Peter not to fight. Jesus knew this was part of God's plan.

Even though Jesus had done nothing wrong, the Roman governor sentenced Jesus to die on a cross. But Jesus didn't stay dead! Three days later, women came to visit His tomb, but Jesus wasn't there. Then Jesus visited His friends and talked with them. Finally, Jesus returned to heaven, where He lives today. Because Jesus died and rose again, we can all become members of God's family and experience His love forever!

Teacher's Devotional

How many times have we promised that our love and friendship would last forever? A childhood friend, a high school sweetheart, a college roommate. Something in us makes us want to pledge to love forever—even if we have done so before and seen that love come to an end. Perhaps this is because we were made by God to give and to receive a love that is true and lasting.

Being created in God's own image endowed us to receive God's love and to love Him in return. God's original plan for us was a love relationship that would last forever. Although this plan was broken through our sin, we still consistently desire to love forever. But we cannot know the true and lasting love God wants us to experience until we receive Jesus Christ as our Lord and our Savior. Only He can remove the sin barrier to open the way to the Father. And although our love frequently falters, God's love never fails.

Before this week is over, make sure every child in your circle of influence understands the reality of God's forever love. Each child needs to know that our desire for a relationship that lasts forever was put there by God. And when we become members of God's family, nothing will ever separate us from His love. What a reward it will be to experience the forever love of heaven with these young ones!

Crafts for Young Children

Craft projects for young children are a blend of "I wanna do it myself!" and "I need help!" Crafts usually require a certain amount of adult assistance—preparing a pattern, doing some cutting, preselecting magazine pictures, tying a knot, etc. But always take care to avoid robbing the child of the satisfaction of his or her own unique efforts. Do only what is absolutely necessary! The adult's desire to have a nice finished project should not override the child's pleasure in experimenting with color and texture. Avoid the temptation to do the project for the child or to improve on his or her efforts.

Some of these crafts have enrichment and simplification ideas. An enrichment idea provides a way to make the craft more challenging for the older child. A simplification idea helps the younger child complete the craft successfully.

Although most projects in this book allow plenty of leeway for children to be creative, some children may become frustrated with the limitations of a structured craft. This frustration may be a signal that the child needs an opportunity to work with more basic, less structured materials: blank paper and markers, play dough, or precut magazine pictures to make into a collage. In any task a young child undertakes, remember that *the process the child goes through is more important than the finished product.*

Happy Clam (15–20 MINUTES)

Materials

- Clam Pattern
- Heart Pattern
- pink card stock
- acrylic pearlized paints in various pastel colors
- spring-type clothespins
- small sponge pieces

For each child—

- 9-inch (23-cm) fluted, white paper plate
- two large wiggle eyes
- large white sequin or fake pearl

Standard Supplies

- pencil
- scissors
- marker
- shallow containers
- newspaper
- glue

Preparation

Fold paper plate in half. Place Clam Pattern on fold. Trace and cut out one clam for each child. With marker write "God's Love is Giving" on the inside of each clam (sketch a). Photocopy onto pink card stock one copy of Heart Pattern for each child. Pour paint into shallow containers. Clip clothespins to sponge pieces to use as handles. Cover work area with newspaper.

TREASURE TALK

Some clams live in thick, large shells. This keeps them safe from other marine animals. God gave every creature a special place for its home. What kind of home did God give you to live in? God gives us many good things because He loves us.

Instruct each child in the following procedures:

- Open the clam. Glue heart to inside of clam (sketch a).
- Open clam and lay flat, with the outside of clam facing up.
- Sponge paint the outside of the clam (sketch b). Use two or three different colors.
- Let clam dry, and then refold card.
- Glue wiggle eyes to the outside "shell" of clam.
- Glue sequin or pearl to inside of clam on the heart.

Enrichment Idea

After sponge painting outside of clam and while paint is still wet, sprinkle iridescent glitter over wet paint.

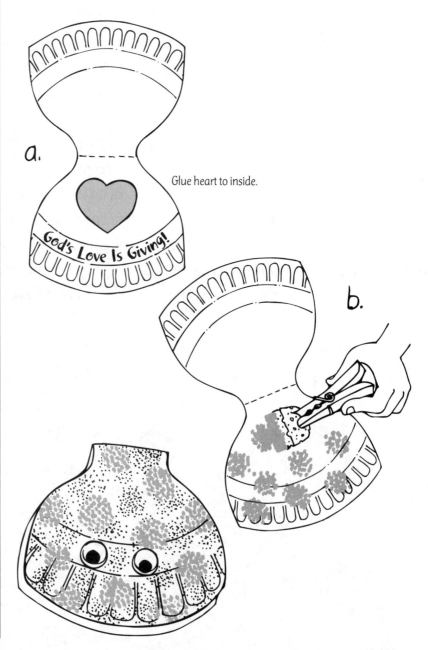

Glue heart to inside.

Clam Pattern

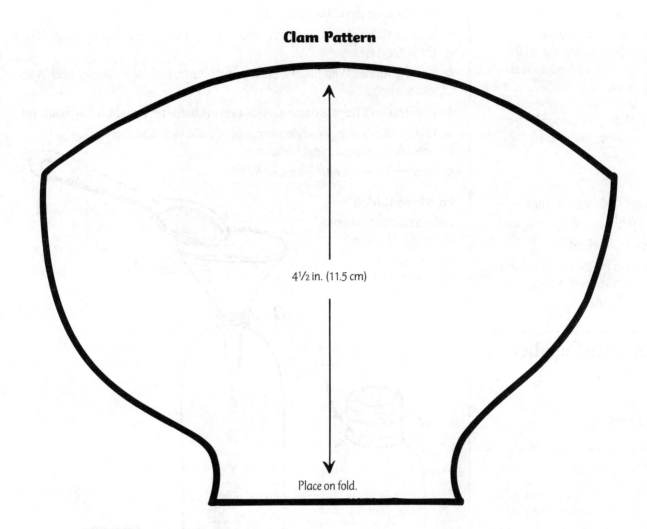

4½ in. (11.5 cm)

Place on fold.

Heart Pattern

Under-the-Sea Shaker (15–20 MINUTES)

Materials

- blow-dryers
- various decorative and noise-making materials (such as colored aquarium gravel, tiny seashells or dyed shell-shaped pasta, green Mylar, fish-shaped plastic confetti, fake pearls)
- funnels
- spoons
- electrical tape in various colors

For each child—

- clear plastic single-serving water or soft-drink bottle with cap

Standard Supplies

- shallow containers
- glue
- scissors

Preparation

Rinse bottles. Use blow-dryer to soften glue and more easily remove labels. Allow to dry. Pour noise-making materials into separate shallow containers.

TREASURE TALK

Annie, thank you for giving the dolphin sticker to Corinne. That was a kind thing to do. Our Bible says, *Love is patient, love is kind* **(1 Corinthians 1:4). What are some other ways you can be kind?**

Instruct each child in the following procedures:

- Set funnel on top of the bottle (sketch a).
- Spoon smaller objects, such as gravel and confetti, into the funnel and let fall into the bottle.
- Remove funnel. With fingers, push larger objects, such as macaroni and Mylar, into the bottle.
- With teacher's help, squeeze glue around the bottle neck and twist on bottle cap.
- With teacher's help, wind electrical tape around neck and cap until cap is secured to neck (sketch b).
- Now shake your bottle back and forth!

Enrichment Idea

Children decorate outside of completed bottles with sea-creature stickers (available from Gospel Light).

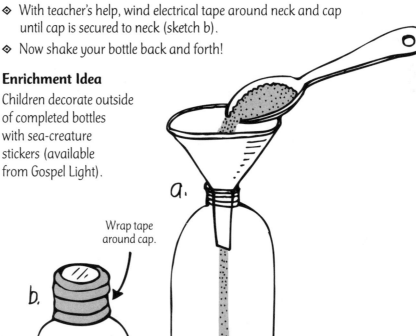

a.

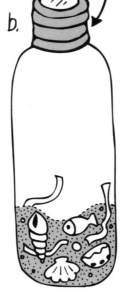

Wrap tape around cap.

b.

Bathtub Boat (10–15 MINUTES)

Materials

- craft foam sheets in various colors
- peel-and-stick geometric foam stickers (available from school supply stores)
- low-temperature glue gun
- permanent markers in various colors

For each child—

- 1-inch (2.5-cm) thick household sponge
- drinking straw

Standard Supplies

- scissors
- ruler
- shallow containers
- hole punch
- glue

Preparation

Cut corners off one end of each sponge (sketch a). Use tip of scissors to poke a hole in the center of sponge large enough for the straw to fit into (sketch a). Cut craft foam into one 4x6-inch (10x15-cm) rectangle for every two children. Then cut rectangles diagonally in half to make two sails (sketch b). Place craft foam stickers in shallow containers. Plug in glue gun out of reach of children.

TREASURE TALK

Katie, you were patient while you waited for the teacher to glue the sail to your boat. God wants us to be patient with others. Our Bible says, *Love is patient, love is kind* (1 Corinthians 13:4). **When we are patient, we are showing God's love. Where will you float your sailboat?**

Instruct each child in the following procedures:

- Use markers to decorate sail.
- Stick craft foam shapes onto sail for additional decoration.
- With teacher's help, punch a hole at the top and the bottom of sail (sketch c).
- Insert straw through the two holes for the mast. Pull sail to top of straw (sketch d).
- Ask a teacher to use glue gun to glue the bottom end of straw into sponge hole (sketch d).

Enrichment Idea

Provide large containers of shallow water or a water table in which children sail their boats.

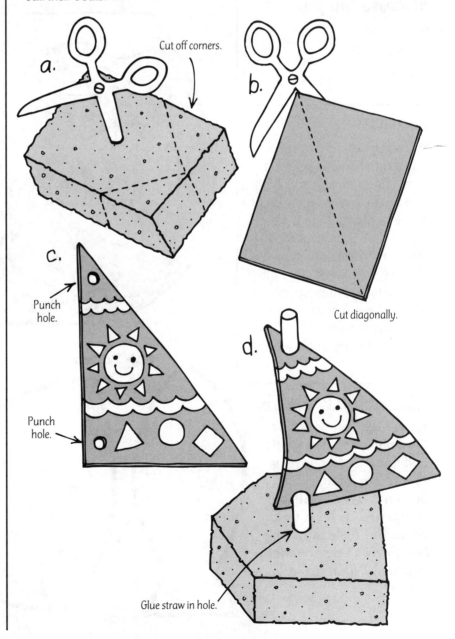

a. Cut off corners.

b. Cut diagonally.

c. Punch hole. Punch hole.

d. Glue straw in hole.

Fishbowl Picture (10–15 MINUTES)

Materials

- Fish Patterns
- Coral Pattern
- Fishbowl Pattern (p. 61)
- card stock in various colors
- green yarn
- blue crayons
- aquarium rocks
- small seashells (available from craft stores)

Standard Supplies

- scissors
- ruler
- glue

Preparation

Photocopy onto card stock several of each Fish and Coral Patterns, making enough for each child to have four or five fish and two pieces of coral. Cut out. Place a piece of white paper over patterns in the middle of Fishbowl Pattern so that they won't be visible, and then photocopy onto card stock one fishbowl for each child. Cut yarn into 3-inch (7.5-cm) pieces to represent seaweed.

TREASURE TALK

Tyler, I see that you chose the yellow fish. I'm glad God loved us and gave us eyes to see pretty colors. God loves us here with our friends and He loves us at home. Our Bible says, *Love lasts forever.* Let's say that together. Repeat verse with children.

Instruct each child in the following procedures:

- Cut out fishbowl.
- Use blue crayons to color fishbowl.
- Glue aquarium rocks to the bottom of fishbowl.
- Glue fish, coral pieces, shells and yarn to fishbowl.

Simplification Idea

Place sand and several plastic spoons in small containers. Children use cotton swabs to spread glue at bottom of fishbowl. With plastic spoons, children sprinkle sand onto glue.

Enrichment Idea

Children decorate fish using colored or glitter glue.

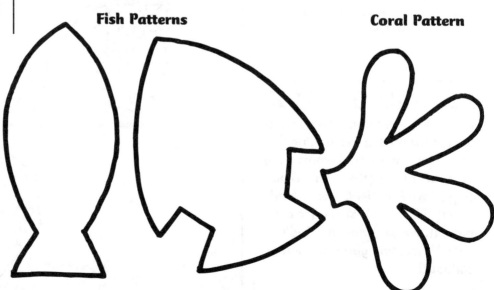

Fish Patterns   **Coral Pattern**

Nativity Scene Diorama (10–15 MINUTES)

Materials

- small saw
- curling ribbon
- various farm animal stickers including sheep and cows
- straw

For each child—

- three large flat wooden clothespins (non-spring type)
- child-sized shoe box
- craft stick broken in half
- two star stickers

Standard Supplies

- scissors
- ruler
- markers
- craft glue
- transparent tape

Preparation

Saw legs on one set of clothespins for each child as shown in sketch a. Cut curling ribbon into one 2-inch (5-cm) length for each child.

TREASURE TALK

Dylan, thank you for sharing the markers and glue with Logan. God gives us many good friends to work with. God loves us. God showed love for us when He sent His Son, Jesus. Our Bible says, *God loved us: He sent His Son*. (See 1 John 4:9.)

Instruct each child in the following procedures:

- Place shoe box on its side to form a stable (sketch b).
- Place animal stickers on back wall of stable.
- Use markers to draw faces and clothes on clothespins to make one Joseph, one Mary and one baby Jesus (sketch c).
- Glue craft-stick halves together in an X-shape to represent a manger (sketch d).
- With teacher's help, glue Joseph and Mary to stable floor. Glue baby Jesus to manger, and glue manger to floor between Mary and Joseph (sketch e).
- To make a hanging star, stick star stickers together with one end of ribbon between them; tape other end of ribbon to stable roof (sketch e).
- Scatter pieces of straw on stable floor.

Enrichment Idea

Older children cut scraps of fabric. They glue fabric around baby Jesus to make a blanket.

Snorkeling Mask (20–30 MINUTES)

Materials

- Snorkel Pattern
- Oval Pattern
- blue cellophane
- brightly colored poster board
- elastic cord
- markers in various colors

For each child—
- one 7-inch (18-cm) white paper plate

Standard Supplies

- pencil
- scissors
- hole punch
- tape
- measuring stick

Preparation

Trace Oval Pattern in the center of each paper plate. Cut out ovals (sketch a). To make holes sturdier, place a small piece of tape on paper plate rim near each end of cut-out oval and punch a hole over tape. Cut blue cellophane into one 3x5-inch (7.5x12.5-cm) rectangle for each child. Trace onto poster board one Snorkel Pattern for each child and cut out. Cut one 14-inch (35.5-cm) length of elastic cord for each child.

TREASURE TALK

Meghan, when you put on your snorkeling mask, what looks different? (Everything looks blue.) **You can pretend that you're snorkeling in the ocean when you wear your mask.**

Thank you for using kind words when Todd took the marker you wanted. I'm glad you didn't try to grab it away from him. Our Bible says, [Love] is not easily angered.

Instruct each child in the following procedures:

- Color mask with markers.
- Tape cellophane rectangle to top of plate, covering the oval opening (sketch a).
- With teacher's help, tie elastic cord to holes on each side of mask, adjusting to fit (sketch b).
- Glue snorkel to side of mask (sketch b).
- Wear mask and look at beach objects!

Simplification Idea
Children use colored plates to make masks instead of coloring.

Enrichment Idea
Older children cut out their own Snorkel Pattern.

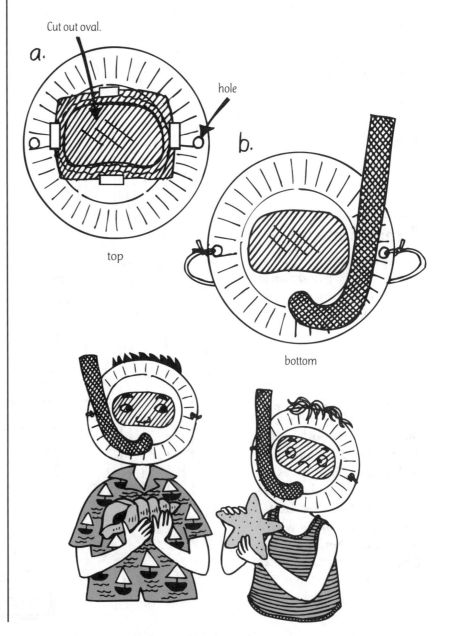

a. Cut out oval.

hole

top

b.

bottom

Snorkel and Oval Patterns

**Snorkel
Pattern**

Oval Pattern

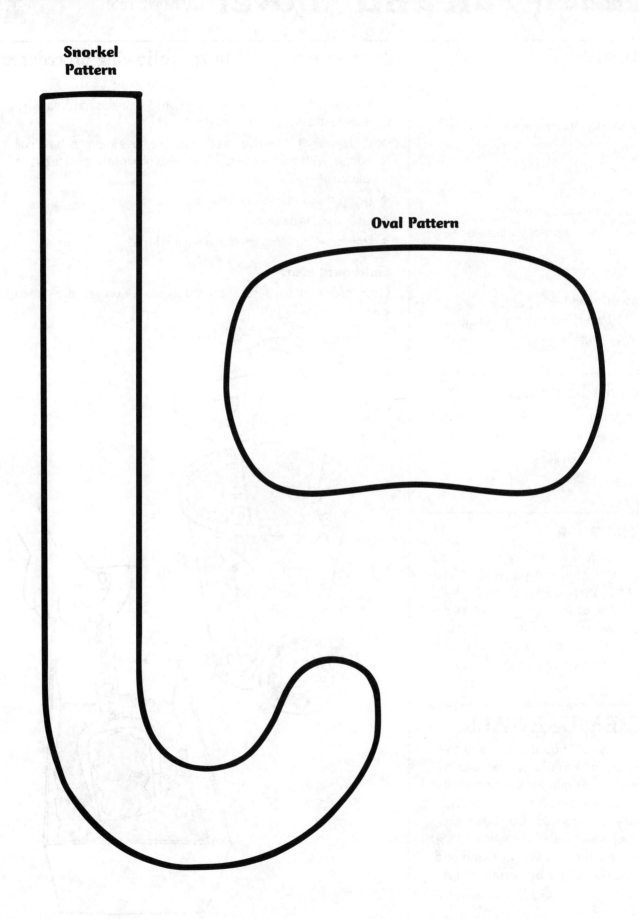

Beach Pail and Shovel (20 MINUTES)

Materials

- ◆ Shovel Pattern
- ◆ Shell Patterns
- ◆ card stock in various colors
- ◆ sand
- ◆ cotton swabs
- ◆ shoe box
- ◆ disposable plastic spoons
- ◆ fish stickers (available from Gospel Light)
- ◆ glitter crayons

For each child—
- ◆ brightly colored 16-oz. plastic cup
- ◆ chenille wire

Standard Supplies

- ◆ hole punch
- ◆ scissors
- ◆ shallow containers
- ◆ glue

Preparation

With hole punch, punch two holes in each cup near the rim on opposite sides (sketch a). Photocopy onto card stock one Shovel Pattern for each child and cut out. Photocopy two or three Shell Patterns onto card stock for each child. Cut out. Pour sand into shallow containers.

TREASURE TALK

What would you like to do at the beach? How could you be kind to someone as you look for seashells? (Give a shell to my friend. Help my little brother dig for a shell.) **Our Bible says, [Love] is not rude** (1 Corinthians 13:5). **That means that you are kind and show God's love by caring about others.**

Instruct each child in the following procedures:

- ◆ Use cotton swab to spread some glue onto shovel.
- ◆ Hold shovel over shoe box. Use a spoon to sprinkle sand onto glue. Shake extra sand into box (sketch b).
- ◆ Push the ends of chenille wire through the holes in cup to make pail handle. With teacher's help, fold up ends of wire and twist to secure (sketch a).
- ◆ Decorate pail with fish stickers.
- ◆ Color shells to decorate.
- ◆ Use shovel to pick up shells and put inside pail.

Enrichment Ideas

Older children cut out paper shells and shovels. Or use real shells (available from Gospel Light).

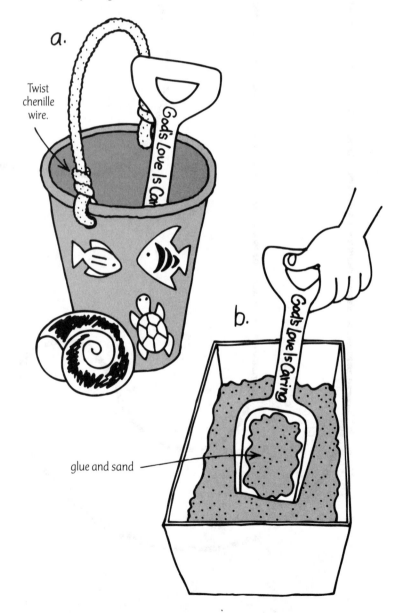

a.

Twist chenille wire.

God's Love Is Caring

b.

God's Love Is Caring

glue and sand

Shovel and Shell Patterns

Shovel Pattern

Shell Patterns

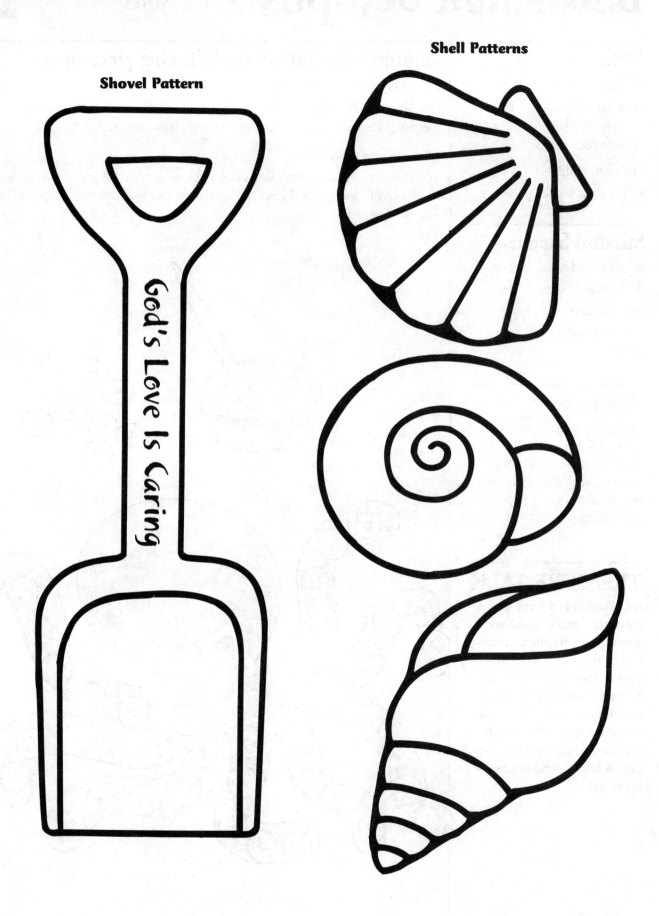

God's Love Is Caring

Decorated Octopus (10–15 MINUTES)

Materials

- Octopus Pattern
- small buttons, large sequins, multi-colored O-shaped cereal
- watercolor paints

For each child—
- two large wiggle eyes

Standard Supplies

- white card stock
- shallow containers
- newspaper
- paintbrushes
- glue

Preparation

Photocopy onto card stock one Octopus Pattern for each child. Put the buttons, sequins and O-shaped cereal in separate shallow containers. Cover work area with newspaper.

TREASURE TALK

An octopus is a kind of sea creature. Jason, what are some other creatures that live in the sea? I'm glad God made all kinds of sea creatures for us to look at. God loves us. God loves us when we are at the beach and God loves us when we are at home. God always loves us!

Instruct each child in the following procedures:

- Paint octopus. Allow to dry.
- Glue eyes onto octopus head.
- Glue buttons, sequins and O-shaped cereal onto octopus arms.

Enrichment Idea

Children trace inside of pattern lines with a colored marker. Fill one small container with water for every four children. Children paint over lines with water to pull color from marker lines.

Octopus Pattern

Young Children • Prekindergarten-Kindergarten

Parrot Glasses (20 MINUTES)

Materials

- ◇ Glasses Pattern
- ◇ Parrot Pattern
- ◇ card stock in various colors
- ◇ craft foam in various colors
- ◇ small paper cups
- ◇ cotton swabs

Standard Supplies

- ◇ scissors
- ◇ stapler
- ◇ pencil
- ◇ hole punch
- ◇ craft glue

Preparation

Photocopy onto card stock one Glasses Pattern for each child. Cut out. Staple sides to front of glasses. Trace two Parrot Patterns onto craft foam for each child. Cut out. Cut foam scraps and use hole punch to make foam dots. Pour craft glue into small cups, one cup for every four children.

TREASURE TALK

Sunglasses help you see better and keep your eyes safe when the sun is bright. I'm glad God gives us good things to keep us from getting hurt or sick. What are some other good things God gives us to help us stay well? (Food. Medicine. Warm clothes.)

Instruct each child in the following procedures:

- ◇ Decorate foam parrot heads by using cotton swabs to glue on foam scraps and dots (sketch a).
- ◇ Spread glue around eyeholes on front of glasses. Press parrot heads onto glasses (sketch b).

Enrichment Idea

With teacher's help, children glue feathers to parrots before gluing onto glasses.

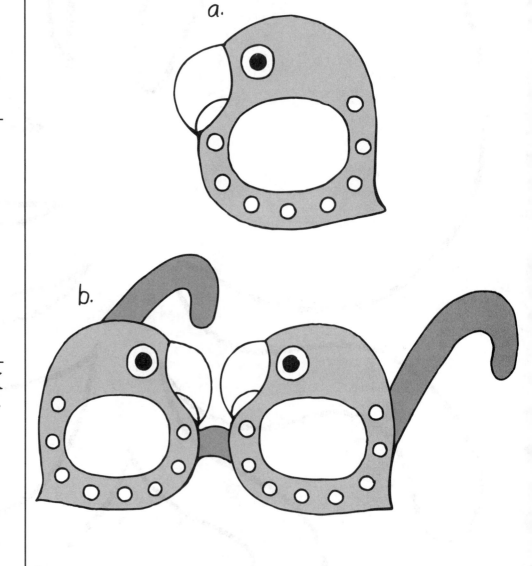

a.

b.

Parrot and Glasses Pattern

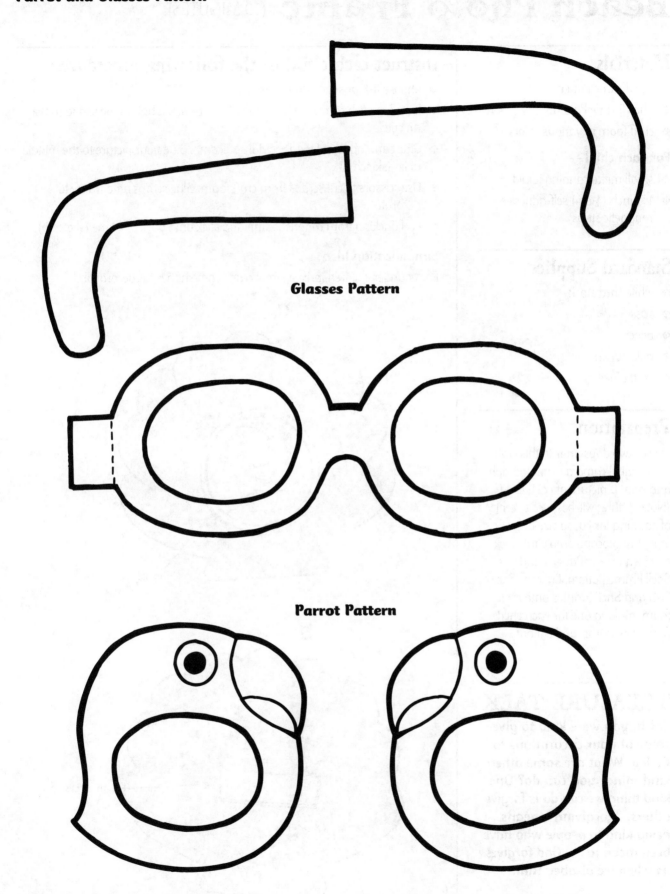

Glasses Pattern

Parrot Pattern

Beach Photo Frame (20 MINUTES)

Materials
- Fish Frame Pattern
- Shell Frame Pattern
- craft foam in various colors

For each child—
- small metal canning jar lid
- 1½-inch (4-cm) self-adhesive magnetic strips

Standard Supplies
- white card stock
- scissors
- pencil
- hole punch
- craft glue

Preparation
One or two days prior to this craft, use a digital camera to photograph and print a picture of each child. (Note: Pictures will be glued to center of canning jar lid, so size accordingly.) Photocopy onto card stock one Fish Frame Pattern and one Shell Frame Pattern. Cut out. Trace Fish and Shell Frames onto craft foam, making one for each child, plus a few extras, and cut out.

TREASURE TALK
Caleb, you were kind to give some of your decorations to Bailey. What are some other kind things you can do? One kind thing we can do is forgive others. "Forgiving" means being kind to people who have been mean to us. God forgives us when we disobey Him.

Instruct each child in the following procedures:
- Choose fish or shell frame to make.
- If making fish frame, with teacher's help, punch a hole in the fish to make an eye.
- Glue canning jar lid to the middle of frame. Glue your picture to the middle of lid (sketch a).
- Use scissors to cut scraps from craft foam. Glue scraps onto frame to decorate.
- Peel backing from magnetic strip and stick onto back of frame (sketch b).

Simplification Idea
For younger children, precut small craft foam shapes for decoration.

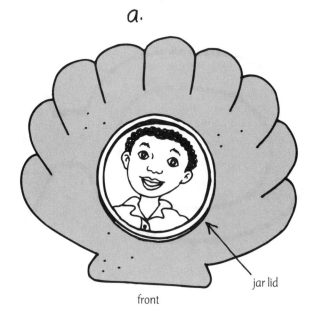

a.

jar lid

front

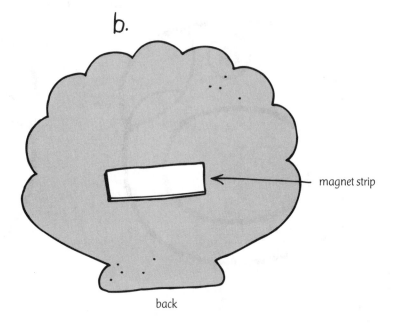

b.

magnet strip

back

Shell Frame and Fish Frame Patterns

Shell Frame Pattern

Fish Frame Pattern

Punch hole.

Love Is Kind Mobile

(ONE- OR TWO-DAY CRAFT/40 MINUTES TOTAL TIME)

Materials

- Heart Patterns
- Sun Mobile Pattern
- Sunglasses Pattern
- card stock in various colors, including yellow
- large kitchen knife
- yellow paper napkins
- yellow yarn or string

For each child—

- 4-inch (10-cm) Styrofoam ball

Standard Supplies

- scissors
- ruler
- craft glue
- shallow containers
- water
- newspaper
- paintbrushes
- colored markers
- hole punches

DAY ONE Preparation

Photocopy Heart Patterns onto colored card stock to make one set for each child plus a few extras. Cut out. With kitchen knife, cut each Styrofoam ball in half. Cut paper napkins into 3-inch (7.5-cm) squares. Pour glue into shallow containers and dilute with small amount of water. Cover work area with newspaper.

Instruct each child in the following procedures:

- Using paintbrush, apply glue to small area of the rounded side of one Styrofoam ball half. Place a napkin square on glued area and carefully brush glue on top to smooth edges down.
- Continue to apply napkin squares, one at a time, to curved side of ball. Overlap the napkin squares until Styrofoam is completely covered. Smooth squares under flat edge of Styrofoam (sketch a).
- Repeat above procedure to decorate other half of ball.
- On the back of each heart, draw a picture of someone you love.

DAY TWO Preparation

Photocopy onto card stock one copy each of Sunglasses Pattern and Sun Mobile Pattern for each child, and cut out. Punch hole in top of Sun Mobile Pattern. Cut three various lengths of yarn or string between approximately 4 inches (10 cm) and 8 inches (20.5 cm) long. Cut a fourth length of yarn or string approximately 6 inches (15 cm) long and thread through the hole at the top of sun, and then knot to make a hanging loop.

Instruct each child in the following procedures:

- Punch a hole in the yellow sun rays where indicated on sun and at the top middle of each heart (sketch b).
- Apply glue to the flat sides of Styrofoam ball halves. Glue the halves to the front and back of card stock sun.
- With teacher's help, tie hearts to the sun in correct word order.
- Glue glasses onto Styrofoam sun.
- Use marker to draw smile on Styrofoam sun.

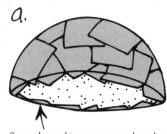

a.

Smooth napkin squares under edge of Styrofoam.

b. Punch holes.

Punch holes.

Love Kind Is

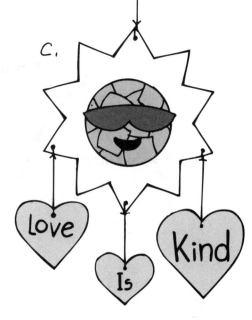

c.

Love Is Kind

TREASURE TALK

Ryan, you were being kind to Kevin when you let him use your paintbrush. We can show love to others when we are kind to them. When has someone been kind to you? Being kind and patient is a way to show God's love to others.

Sun Mobile and Sunglasses Patterns

Sun Mobile Pattern

Sunglasses Pattern

Young Children • Prekindergarten-Kindergarten

Young Children • Prekindergarten-Kindergarten

© 2006 Gospel Light. Permission to photocopy granted. *Island Crafts for Kids*

Zacchaeus Puppet Theater

(15–20 MINUTES)

Materials

- Zacchaeus Puppet Pattern
- Jesus Puppet Pattern
- brown paper bags
- nature stickers
- resealable plastic sandwich bags

For every two children—
- sheet of green poster board

For each child—
- two tongue depressors

Standard Supplies

- scissors
- white card stock
- glue
- crayons
- tape

Preparation

Cut one sheet of poster board in half width-wise so that you have one half for each child. Cut the top of each half to look like trees (sketch a). Fold each side of board to meet in the middle. Photocopy one set of Zacchaeus and Jesus Puppet Patterns onto card stock for each child. Cut out three tree trunk shapes from paper bags for each child.

TREASURE TALK

Zacchaeus had done many wrong things. He wanted to see Jesus, but he was a short man, so he climbed up in a tree. What did Jesus say to Zacchaeus when He saw him in the tree? ("Zacchaeus, I want to go to your house today.") **Zacchaeus was sorry for the wrong things he had done. Jesus forgave Zacchaeus because He loved Zacchaeus. Jesus loves us, too.** Our Bible says, **[Love] is not easily angered** (1 Corinthians 13:5).

Instruct each child in the following procedures:

- Glue tree trunks to the poster-board puppet theater (sketch a).
- Place nature stickers on scene.
- Color Zacchaeus and Jesus. Cut out Zacchaeus and Jesus.
- Glue Zacchaeus and Jesus to tongue depressors to make puppets (sketch b).
- Tape sides of plastic bag to back of poster board theater (sketch c). Keep puppets in bag so they won't get lost.
- Use your puppet theater to tell your friends or family the story of Zacchaeus!

Enrichment Idea

Older children cut out their own tree trunk shapes. They glue dried leaves to trees.

a. Fold.

Glue tree trunks.

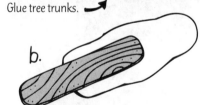

b.

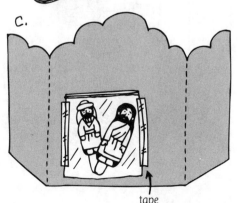

c.

tape

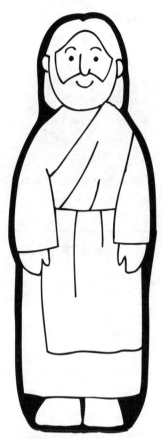

Jesus and Zacchaeus Puppet Patterns

Woman at the Well (10–15 MINUTES)

Materials

- Backdrop Pattern
- Jesus Pattern
- Woman Pattern
- poster board
- tan card stock
- brown craft foam
- double-stick tape

For every three children—
- toilet paper tube

Standard Supplies

- pencil
- scissors
- craft knife
- ruler
- glue
- shallow containers
- crayons or markers
- stapler

Preparation

Enlarge Backdrop Pattern to 200 percent and trace onto poster board to make one pattern for each child. Cut out. Fold poster board on dashed lines and then reopen. Photocopy onto the cardstock one Woman Pattern and one Jesus Pattern for each child and cut out. Use craft knife to cut slot where indicated on Backdrop Pattern. Cut craft foam into one ½x8-inch (1.3x20.5-cm) strip for each child. Cut toilet paper tubes into thirds. Pour glue into shallow containers.

Instruct each child in the following procedures:

- Use markers to draw clouds, tree and sky on top portion of poster board backdrop (sketch a).
- Color the bottom portion to look like the ground.
- Ask teacher to fold and staple poster board (sketch b).
- With teacher's help, wrap double-stick tape to sides of toilet paper tube (sketch c).
- Cut foam strip into small pieces and stick to tape to form bricks on a well.
- Dip one end of well into white glue and set on bottom right side of picture (sketch b).
- Using crayons or markers, color Jesus and Woman figures.
- Use double-stick tape to attach Jesus figure to backdrop near well (sketch d).
- Insert the tab of Woman Pattern into slot. Use the tab to move Woman toward the well.

Simplification Ideas

Tape already-colored Jesus and Woman Patterns to sides of overturned 3-ounce disposable cups (plastic or unwaxed paper). Glue small cereal squares to well for bricks instead of using craft foam.

Enrichment Ideas

Older children cut out their own Jesus and Woman Patterns. Crumple small pieces of blue tissue paper and put in well to make water.

a.

c.
tape

b.
Glue well here.
Staple.

d.

Jesus and Woman Patterns

Jesus
Pattern

Woman
Pattern

tab

TREASURE TALK
Zachary, I see that you are sharing the tape with Emmit. God helps us show His love by sharing with others. Who are some people at your home that you can share with? (Little sister. Dad. Grandma.) **I'm glad God loves us and helps us show love to our friends and family.**

Young Children • Prekindergarten-Kindergarten

Backdrop Pattern

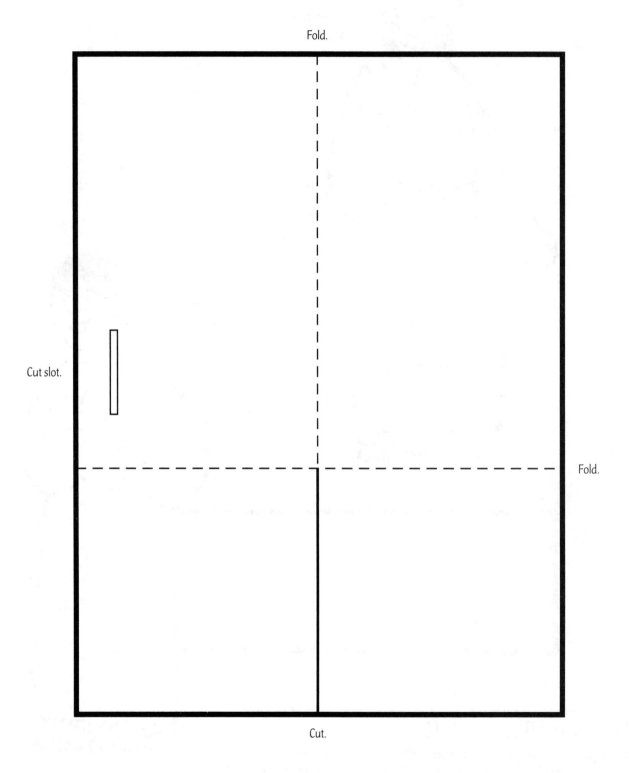

Fold.

Cut slot.

Fold.

Cut.

Loving Treasure Chest (15–20 MINUTES)

Materials

- brown watercolor markers
- acrylic gems (available from Gospel Light)
- magazines

For each child—

- plastic baby-wipe box with flip-up lid

Standard Supplies

- masking tape
- shallow containers
- water
- foam paintbrushes
- glue
- scissors

Preparation

Tear masking tape into approximately 4-inch (10-cm) lengths and place along the sides of the table. Fill shallow containers with water.

TREASURE TALK

What pictures did you put in your chest, Mia? What do you like best about your (house)? God cares about us. He gives us homes and families to keep us safe.

Instruct each child in the following procedures:

- Cover top and all four sides of box with overlapping pieces of masking tape (sketch a).
- Use markers to color masking tape pieces.
- Dip paintbrushes in water and paint a small amount of water over colored masking tape (sketch b). This will cause marker ink to spread and will make tape appear leather-like.
- Glue gems to outside of chest (sketch c).
- Cut pictures of things you love from magazines and put inside your chest.

Enrichment Idea
Children tear their own masking tape pieces.

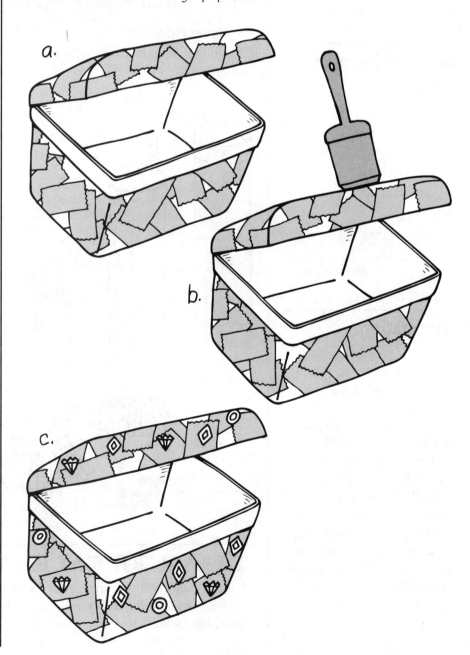

Good News Treasure Carriers

(25–30 MINUTES)

Materials

- metallic-gold spray paint
- yarn
- leatherlike cording
- fringed fabric trim
- assorted acrylic gems (available from Gospel Light)

For each child—

- paper towel tube
- sheet of white paper

Standard Supplies

- newspaper
- scissors
- measuring stick
- marker
- craft glue
- shallow containers
- water
- masking tape
- hole punch
- crayons

Preparation

Cover outdoor work area with newspaper. Spray-paint each paper towel tube. Cut yarn into several 6-inch (15-cm) lengths for each child. Cut cording into one 2-foot (.6-m) length for each child. Cut fringe into one 6-inch (15-cm) length for each child. Write "God Loves Me Forever" at the top of a sheet of white paper and photocopy, making one copy for each child. Pour glue into shallow containers and dilute with a small amount of water.

Instruct each child in the following procedures:

- With teacher's help, criss-cross two pieces of masking tape at one end of tube (sketch a).
- Glue fringe around taped end of tube, hiding tape ends (sketch b).
- With teacher's help, punch two holes at top of Treasure Carrier (sketch c).
- With teacher's help, tie ends of leather cording through each hole.
- Dip yarn pieces into diluted glue and wind around carrier. Glue acrylic gems to carrier (sketch d).
- On the white paper and under the words "God Loves Me Forever," draw a picture of yourself.
- Roll up the picture and place inside your Treasure Carrier.

Enrichment Idea

Children use collage materials to decorate pictures.

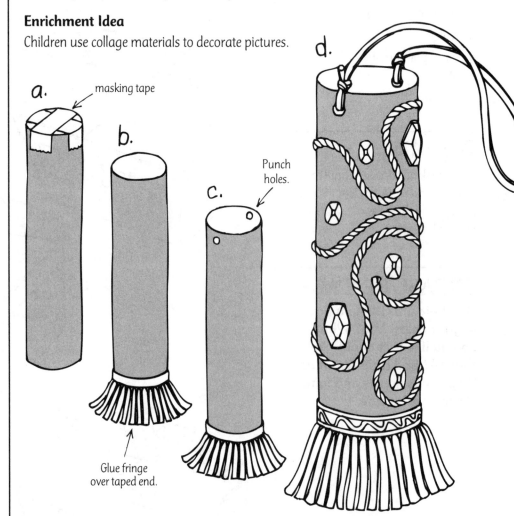

a. masking tape

b.

c. Punch holes.

d.

Glue fringe over taped end.

TREASURE TALK

Aubrey, who will you give your message to? I am glad that God showed His love for us by making Jesus alive again. Our Bible says, *Love lasts forever* (see 1 Corinthians 13:7). God's love never stops.

Section Two/Grades 1-3

Crafts for Younger Elementary

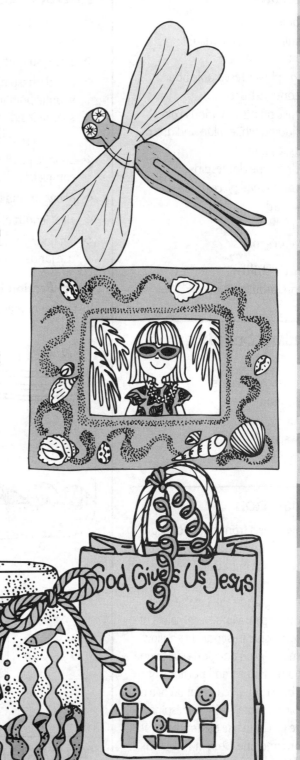

Children in the first few years of school delight in completing craft projects. They have a handle on most of the basic skills needed, they are eager to participate, and their taste in art has usually not yet surpassed their ability to produce. In other words, they generally like what they make.

Because reading ability is not a factor in most craft projects, crafts can be a great leveler among children. Some children who are not top achievers in other areas excel here.

You may find additional projects suitable for younger elementary children in the first section of this book, "Crafts for Young Children."

Scented Seascape Jar (25–30 MINUTES)

Materials

- rubbing alcohol
- small seashells (available from craft stores)
- large plastic resealable bag
- coconut extract
- acrylic paints in various colors, including white, blue and green
- plastic plates
- spring-type clothespins
- small sponge pieces
- jute cord
- sand
- several spoons

For each child—
- clean baby food jar

Standard Supplies

- glue
- shallow containers
- scissors
- ruler
- newspaper
- thin paintbrushes

Preparation

Remove labels from baby food jars using rubbing alcohol. Wash and dry shells and put in plastic resealable bag. Pour the entire bottle of extract into the bag and seal. Let the shells soak overnight. Mix several colors of paint and glue in separate shallow containers, using one part glue to one part paint. Pour small portions of white, blue and green paint on two or three plastic plates. Clip clothespins to sponge pieces to use as handles. Cut jute cord into one 12-inch (30.5-cm) length for each child. Dip ends of jute cord in glue to prevent fraying. Pour sand and seashells into separate shallow containers. Cover work area with newspaper.

Instruct each child in the following procedures:

- Spoon about 1½ inches (4 cm) of sand into the jar. Add a layer of shells (sketch a).
- Screw lid onto jar.
- Use clothespin and sponge to lightly sponge white paint onto jar. Repeat sponge painting with blue and green paint, leaving some areas unpainted so that inside of jar is visible (sketch b).
- Use thin paintbrushes to paint seaweed, fish, coral and bubbles on jar.
- Sponge paint the jar lid with white, blue and green paint, covering lid completely.
- Allow jar and lid to dry.
- Tie a length of jute around the lid (sketch c).
- Set your Seascape Jar in a bathroom or your room and unscrew the lid to use jar as a room freshener.

Simplification Idea

Instead of painting, children decorate jar using vellum fish and marine animal stickers.

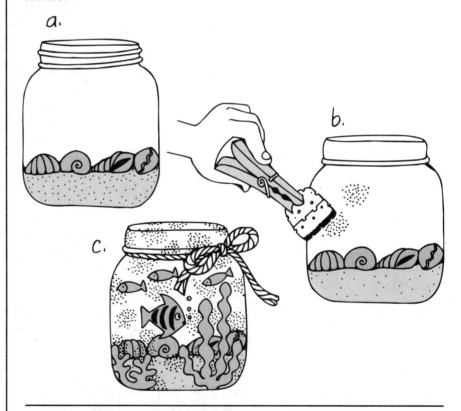

a.

b.

c.

TREASURE TALK

When you set your Seascape Jar in a room and take off the lid, it will make the room smell good. You can give your jar to someone you love. What are some other ways you can show love to someone? Sometimes we give gifts to the people we love. Because God loves us, He gave us a very special gift. He sent His Son, Jesus!

Clothespin Dragonfly (25–30 MINUTES)

Materials

- Dragonfly Wings Pattern
- vellum sheets
- blue and green acrylic paint
- low-temperature glue gun
- glitter pens

For each child—
- round-headed wooden clothespin (non-spring type)
- two sequins

Standard Supplies

- pencil
- scissors
- shallow containers
- newspaper
- paintbrushes
- glue

Preparation

Trace one Dragonfly Wing Pattern onto vellum for each child. Cut between patterns to separate, but don't cut out. Pour paint into shallow containers. Cover work area with newspaper. Plug in glue gun out of reach of children.

TREASURE TALK

Dragonflies have big eyes that are really thousands of tiny eyes packed together. This helps them see movement up to 50 feet (15 m) away and helps protect them from their enemies. God cares about the needs of all of His creatures. He especially cares about you! What are some things God has given to help take care of you? (Home. Food. Clothing. Medicine.) **God loves you. His love is caring.**

Instruct each child in the following procedures:

- Paint clothespin to represent dragonfly. Let dry.
- Cut out dragonfly wings.
- Use glitter pens to draw veins on wings.
- Glue sequins onto head to represent eyes.
- With teacher's help, use glue gun to glue wings to back of dragonfly as shown in sketch.

Enrichment Idea

Children twist together three lengths of chenille wire to form six legs. They use craft glue to attach legs to body.

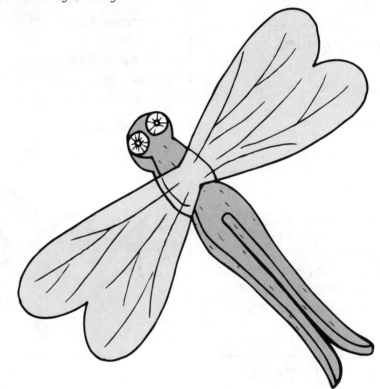

Dragonfly Wings Pattern

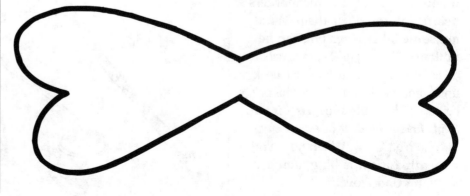

Big Catch Game (25–30 MINUTES)

Materials

- Big Fish Pattern
- permanent markers in various colors, including black
- craft foam
- jute cord or string

For each child—

- three canning jar rings or plastic bracelets at least 2 inches (5 cm) in diameter
- 14-inch (35.5-cm) long stick

Standard Supplies

- scissors
- measuring stick
- hole punch
- craft glue
- tape

Preparation

With marker, trace two Big Fish Patterns onto craft foam for each child. Cut between patterns to separate, but don't cut out. Cut a 2-inch (5-cm) circle in the center of each fish (sketch a). Cut the jute cord or string into 20-inch (51-cm) lengths.

TREASURE TALK

There were many steps involved in making your game. It took time and patience to finish making it. Many of you had to wait for your friends to finish using the markers before you could use them. What are some other ways you can be patient? (Waiting for a turn to get a drink. Waiting to look at the ocean book until someone else has finished his or her turn.) **The Bible says, Love is patient, love is kind. It does not envy** (1 Corinthians 13:4). **When you wait patiently for something, you are showing God's love.**

Instruct each child in the following procedures:

- Cut out two Big Fish.
- Lay fish so they face opposite directions (sketch a). Outline both fish with black marker. Draw an eye on each fish.
- Color fish with patterns such as stripes, dots and curvy lines.
- Punch a hole in the mouth end of each fish (sketch a).
- Glue a canning jar ring or plastic bracelet to the back of one fish, framing the hole in the fish. Then glue the back of the other fish onto the opposite side of ring or bracelet, so ring is between fish (sketch b).
- Tie one end of cord or string about 1 inch (2.5 cm) from one end of stick. Wrap tape over knot to secure (sketch c).
- Thread the opposite end of cord through the punched holes on fish and tie a knot.
- Thread two canning jar rings over the stick and onto the string.
- To play the game, hold the end of the stick and swing the fish. The object is to catch the two rings on the end of the stick, and then catch the fish.

Enrichment Idea

Children wrap the stick with colored electrical tape stripes to decorate.

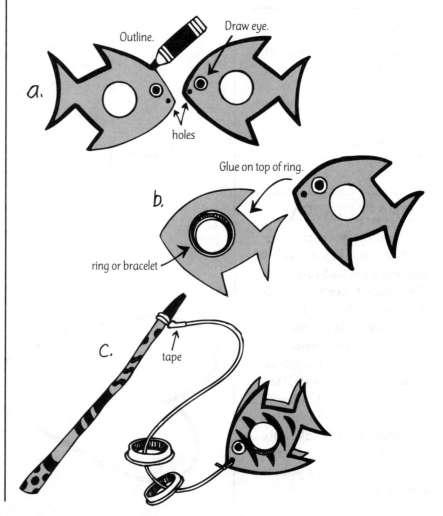

a. Outline. Draw eye. holes

b. Glue on top of ring. ring or bracelet

c. tape

Younger Elementary • Grades 1-3

Big Fish Pattern

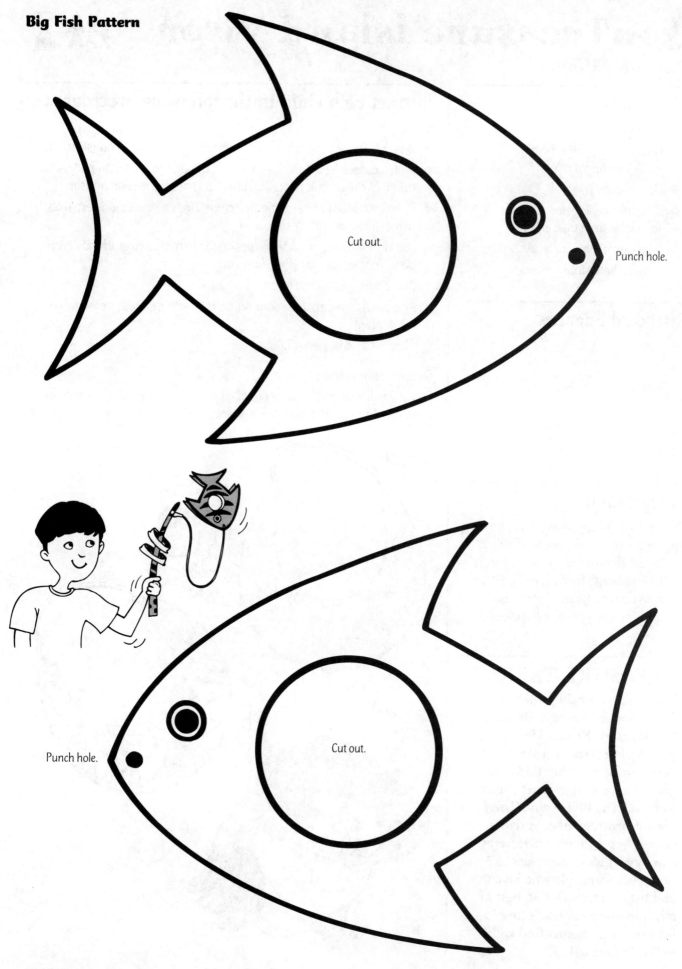

Cut out.

Punch hole.

Punch hole.

Cut out.

Younger Elementary • Grades 1-3

SonTreasure Island Visor

(25–30 MINUTES)

Materials

- ◆ Visor Pattern
- ◆ craft foam or poster board in various bright colors
- ◆ elastic cord
- ◆ assorted acrylic gems (available from Gospel Light)
- ◆ permanent markers or glitter pens
- ◆ squeeze-bottle fabric paints

Standard Supplies

- ◆ pencil
- ◆ scissors
- ◆ ruler
- ◆ newspaper
- ◆ hole punch
- ◆ glue

Preparation

Trace Visor Pattern onto craft foam or poster board to make one visor for each child. Cut elastic cord into one 12-inch (30.5-cm) length for each child. Set out remaining craft foam or poster board scraps. Cover work area with newspaper.

TREASURE TALK

Your visor can help protect your face from the hot sun. Because God loves us, He provides many things to protect us from harm. What are some other things God gives you to protect you? (Parents. Teachers.) **The Bible says, [Love] always protects, always trusts, always hopes, always perseveres. Love never fails** (1 Corinthians 13:7-8). **God gives us people who love us and help protect us. But, best of all, God loves us. God's love is forever. That means God will ALWAYS love us!**

Instruct each child in the following procedures:

- ◆ Cut out visor.
- ◆ With hole punch, punch a hole near each end of visor band (sketch a).
- ◆ With teacher's help, thread elastic cord through the holes and adjust length of elastic to fit head. Tie cord in a knot on each end of visor.
- ◆ From craft foam or poster board scraps, cut out small triangles, ovals, wavy stripes and other shapes.
- ◆ Lay visor flat and arrange shapes on top to make sea or island decorations. Glue shapes to visor (sketch b).
- ◆ Glue acrylic gems onto visors.
- ◆ Add details (stripes, dots, your name, etc.) with markers, pens and/or fabric paint.
- ◆ Allow visor to dry overnight.

Simplification Idea

Precut small geometric shapes out of craft foam or construction paper, or purchase die-cut craft foam sticker shapes.

Visor Pattern

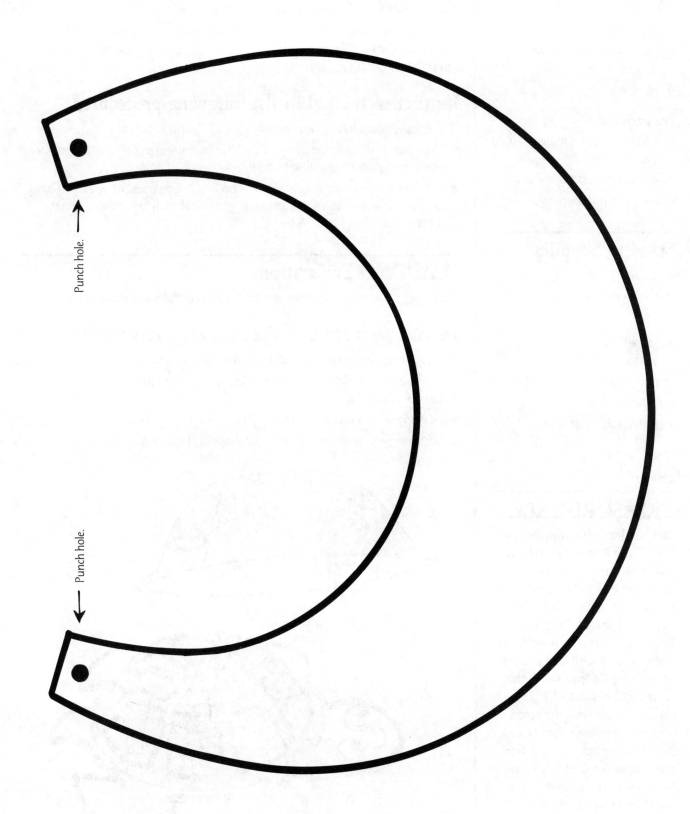

Punch hole.

Punch hole.

Salty the Sea Turtle
(TWO-DAY CRAFT/35–40 MINUTES TOTAL TIME)

Materials

- Sea Turtle Pattern
- green tissue paper in various shades
- black markers

For each child—
- one 6-inch (15-cm) heavy-duty paper bowl
- one green craft foam sheet
- two 18-mm wiggle eyes

Standard Supplies

- glue
- shallow containers
- water
- newspaper
- scissors
- paintbrushes
- pencils
- lightweight cardboard

TREASURE TALK

Sea turtles have flippers for feet. They live in the ocean but crawl up on the beach to lay their eggs. The mother turtle digs a hole, lays her eggs and then buries them. When it is time to hatch, the baby turtles wait until night-time. Why do you think they wait until it's dark? (So they can safely crawl into the ocean and hide from crabs and birds that like to eat baby turtles.) **God cares about all of His creatures and helps them have what they need. He especially cares about us!**

DAY ONE Preparation

Pour glue into shallow containers and dilute with water. Cover work area with newspaper. Cut sample-sized square from tissue paper and show to children before they begin cutting squares.

Instruct each child in the following procedures:

- Cut tissue paper into approximately 3-inch (7.5-cm) squares.
- With paintbrush, spread a coat of glue over a small area of the outside of the bowl. Apply a square of tissue and brush with glue again.
- Continue applying tissue squares, overlapping as you go, until outside of bowl is completely covered. At the bottom edge of bowl, turn tissue edges under (sketch a).

DAY TWO Preparation

Trace several Sea Turtle Patterns onto lightweight cardboard and cut out.

Instruct each child in the following procedures:

- Trace turtle shape onto the craft foam with marker and cut out.
- Use marker to outline turtle shape. Draw the turtle's mouth. Draw squares on its shell (sketch b).
- Glue wiggle eyes on turtle's head.
- Center turtle shell on craft foam turtle shape and glue together.

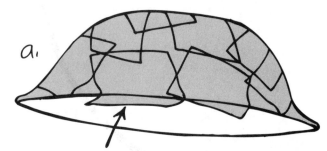

a.

Turn tissue under edge.

b.

Sea Turtle Pattern

Sandy Shore Picture Frame

(15–20 MINUTES)

Materials

- blue poster board
- heavy cardboard
- low-temperature glue gun
- large shallow box or container
- sand
- small seashells (available from craft stores)

For every two children—
- 12-inch (30.5-cm) chenille wire

Standard Supplies

- scissors
- ruler
- craft knife
- glue

Preparation

Cut poster board into one 6x8-inch (15x20.5-cm) rectangle for each child. With craft knife and ruler, cut out a window in the center of each poster board piece, slightly smaller than 3 inches (7.5 cm). With craft knife, cut heavy cardboard into one 6x8-inch (15x20.5-cm) rectangle for each child. Cut chenille wire into one 6-inch (15-cm) length for each child. Plug in glue gun out of reach of children.

TREASURE TALK

Whose picture are you going to put in your frame? God takes care of us by giving us special people who love us. When you look at the picture in your frame, you can remember that your (dad) loves you and that God loves you, too! The Bible says, [Love] always protects, always trusts, always hopes, always perseveres. Love never fails (1 Corinthians 13:7-8). **God's love is forever!**

Instruct each child in the following procedures:

- Decide which way you'd like your picture frame to hang, and then glue poster board frame to heavy cardboard back. Glue only the sides and bottom of frame. Keep glue away from photo opening at top of frame (sketch a).
- Bend chenille wire to form picture hanger (sketch b). With teacher's help, use glue gun to glue hanger to back of frame.
- Squeeze glue in wavy patterns near the bottom and sides of frame (sketch c).
- Place frame in shallow box and sprinkle sand over the glued areas. Shake excess sand into the box.
- Lay frame flat. Arrange and glue on shells.
- Allow frame to dry flat several hours.
- Slide your favorite photo through the opening at top of frame.

Enrichment Idea

One or two days before craft, use a digital camera to photograph and print individual or group photos of children in front of a tropical or seaside backdrop. Children insert photos into completed frames.

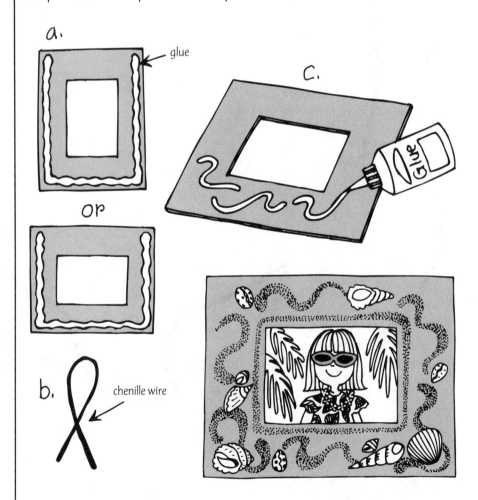

a.   glue

or

b.   chenille wire

c.   Glue

Sand Painting (25–30 MINUTES)

Materials

- ◆ construction paper in various colors
- ◆ margarine tubs with lids
- ◆ sand
- ◆ powdered tempera paint in various colors
- ◆ large containers
- ◆ clear acrylic spray

For each child—
- ◆ one sheet of black sandpaper
- ◆ plastic spoon
- ◆ gummed picture hanger

Standard Supplies

- ◆ scissors
- ◆ newspaper
- ◆ pencils
- ◆ white glue in squeeze bottles

Preparation

For each child, cut construction paper into one rectangular piece that is 1 inch (2.5 cm) larger on each side than sandpaper sheets. Cover work area with newspaper. Fill margarine tubs one-half to two-thirds full of sand, using one tub for each color of sand. To color sand, add a spoonful of powdered tempera, put on lid and shake sand and tempera together, mixing thoroughly. Add more tempera as needed for desired color intensity. Designate an empty container for each color of sand.

TREASURE TALK

Have you ever visited an island? Because He loves us, God created beautiful places like islands for people to enjoy. What is another way God has shown His love for us? God also showed His love for us when He sent His Son. The Bible says, *This is how God showed his love among us: He sent his one and only son into the world* **(1 John 4:9).**

Instruct each child in the following procedures:

- ◆ Use a pencil to draw simple designs, such as an island with a palm tree, onto black side of sandpaper.
- ◆ Glue sandpaper, black side up, to center of a construction paper sheet.
- ◆ Use glue to trace over lines of picture drawn on sandpaper (sketch a). Only squeeze glue on the parts that you want to be the same color. Fill in outlines with glue if desired.
- ◆ Spoon a small amount of one color of sand over glue (sketch b).
- ◆ Turn picture on edge and tap lightly over designated container to remove excess sand (sketch c).
- ◆ Repeat process for each color of sand to be used.
- ◆ When picture is dry, ask teacher to spray with clear acrylic spray in a well-ventilated area.
- ◆ Apply gummed picture hanger to back.

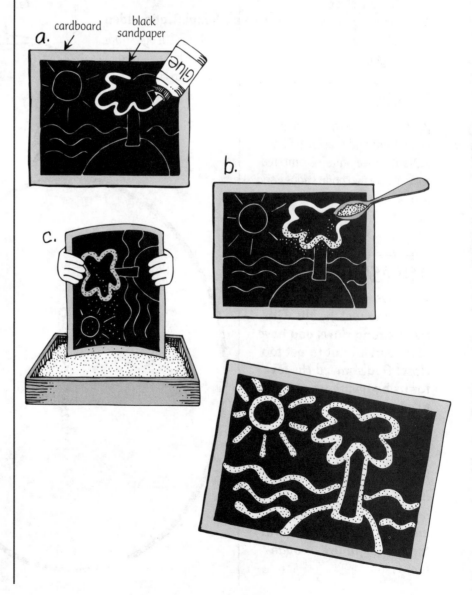

Beanbag Crab (20–25 MINUTES)

Materials
- Crab Body Pattern
- Crab Claw Pattern
- marker
- red or orange felt
- dried beans or aquarium gravel

For each child—
- two wiggle eyes

Optional—
- red staples (available at stationery stores)

Standard Supplies
- white card stock
- scissors
- staplers
- craft glue

Preparation
Photocopy onto card stock one Crab Body and one Crab Claw Pattern. Trace patterns onto red felt to make two body shapes and two claw shapes for each child.

TREASURE TALK
Who has seen a crab? Crabs are fun to watch, but with those strong claws you have to be careful not to get too close! God showed His love for us by giving us a world filled with all sorts of interesting creatures. God loves us so much that He gave us something even more important. The Bible says, *This is how God showed his love among us: He sent his one and only Son into the world that we might live through him* (1 John 4:9).

Instruct each child in the following procedures:
- Cut out crab body and claw shapes.
- Place crab bodies on top of each other, matching edges. Position claws between body shapes as shown in sketch a. Staple claws to body. (Optional: Use the red staples.)
- Staple body together between claws and along sides (sketch b). (Note: Place the staples about ⅛ [.3 cm] inch from edge so that filling doesn't fall out. For extra security, you may want to squeeze a thin line of glue around edge before stapling.) Leave back of crab open.
- Loosely fill crab body with beans or aquarium gravel.
- Staple back edges of crab together to close (sketch c).
- Children glue wiggle eyes onto crab.

Simplification Idea
Children cut eye shapes from felt pieces and glue onto crabs.

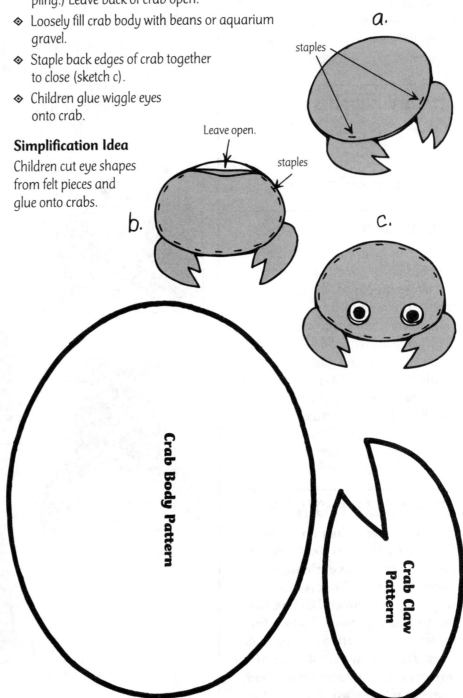

a.

staples

Leave open.

staples

b.

c.

Crab Body Pattern

Crab Claw Pattern

Younger Elementary • Grades 1-3

Seashell Necklace (15–20 MINUTES)

Materials

- Shell Patterns
- card stock in various bright colors
- thin, leather-like lacing
- hair gel
- iridescent glitter
- natural beads (wooden, shell, stone, etc.)
- plastic beads
- metallic beads

(Note: Beads should have openings large enough to thread onto lacing.)

Standard Supplies

- scissors
- measuring stick
- wide paintbrushes
- shallow containers
- hole punch
- masking tape

Preparation

Photocopy five Shell Patterns onto card stock for each child. Cut leather-like lacing into one 1-yard (.9-m) length for each child. With a paintbrush, mix hair gel and iridescent glitter in shallow containers.

TREASURE TALK

Marta, what color is the shell you are painting? I see you chose blue beads for your necklace. What would you have done if someone else took the beads you wanted? You could get angry with the person who took the beads, or you could pick other beads. The Bible says, [Love] is not easily angered, it keeps no record of wrongs (1 Corinthians 13:5-6). **Keeping a record of wrongs is like making a list of the ways others are unkind. That's not a way to show God's love! God forgives us and wants us to forgive others, too.**

Instruct each child in the following procedures:

- Cut out shell patterns.
- Punch a hole in the top of each card stock shell.
- With paintbrush or fingers, paint thin layer of gel mixture on shells. Allow to dry. (Note: Card stock shells may curl slightly, but will flatten when thoroughly dry.)
- Thread shells and beads evenly on the lacing as shown in sketch.
- Tie ends of lacing in a knot.

Enrichment Idea

Photocopy extra shells, and cut smaller pieces of lacing. Children make bracelets to match necklaces.

Shell Patterns

Fishbowl Tic-Tac-Toe (15–20 MINUTES)

Materials

- ❖ Starfish Pattern
- ❖ Angelfish Pattern
- ❖ Fishbowl Pattern
- ❖ blue card stock
- ❖ rickrack in bright colors
- ❖ poster board
- ❖ aquarium gravel
- ❖ craft foam in two bright colors
- ❖ double-stick tape

For each child—
- ❖ 9x12-inch (23x30.5-cm) sheet of yellow construction paper
- ❖ resealable plastic sandwich bag

Standard Supplies

- ❖ scissors
- ❖ measuring stick
- ❖ shallow containers
- ❖ glue
- ❖ hole punch

Preparation

Photocopy onto card stock one Starfish and Angelfish Pattern for every two children. Cut out. Cut rickrack into four 7-inch (18-cm) lengths for each child. Cut the poster board into one 11x14-inch (28x35.5-cm) rectangle for each child. (Hint: Two pieces can be cut from one 22x28-inch [56x71-cm] sheet of poster board). Use pieces of white paper to cover all patterns except square, and then photocopy one Fishbowl Pattern onto blue card stock for each child. Pour aquarium gravel into shallow containers.

TREASURE TALK

What kinds of games do you like to play, Devon? What is a way that you can show love when you play games with your friends? (Invite my friend to go first. Let my friend choose the game we play. Play fairly.) **When you are kind and let your friend play first you are showing God's love.**

Instruct each child in the following procedures:

- ❖ Glue yellow paper to center of poster board.
- ❖ Cut out fish bowl and glue to center of yellow paper (sketch a).
- ❖ Using square as center, glue rickrack to fish bowl to make Tic-Tac-Toe game board (sketch b).
- ❖ Trace Starfish Pattern onto one color craft foam five times. Cut out.
- ❖ Trace Angelfish Pattern onto second color of craft foam five times. Cut out. Punch a hole in each foam fish to make an eye.
- ❖ Use double-stick tape to attach resealable sandwich bag to back of poster board. Store foam shapes in bag when play is completed.
- ❖ Play Tic-Tac-Toe with a friend!

Simplification Idea

Precut starfish and angelfish or use precut fish and star craft-foam shapes (available at craft stores).

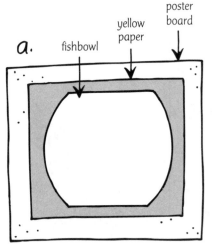

a. fishbowl yellow paper poster board

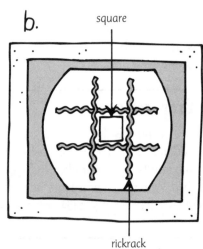

b. square rickrack

Fishbowl, Angelfish and Starfish Patterns

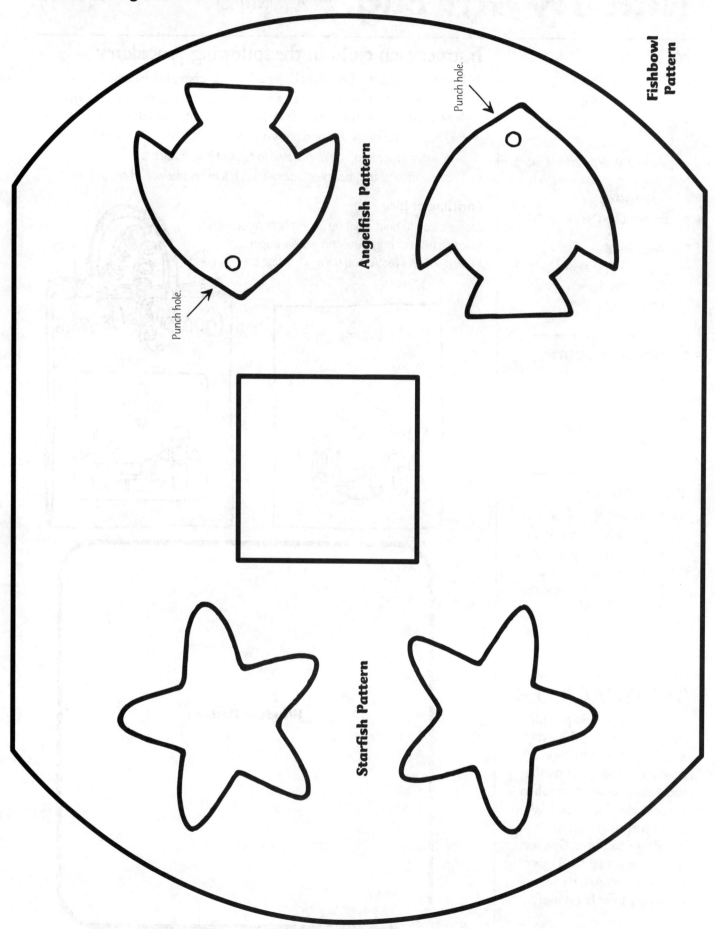

Fishbowl Pattern

Angelfish Pattern

Punch hole.

Punch hole.

Starfish Pattern

Nativity Gift Bag (20–25 MINUTES)

Materials

- Window Pattern
- brown craft foam
- permanent fine-tip markers in various colors
- peel-and-stick geometric foam stickers (available from school supply stores)
- curling ribbon

For each child—

- 5½x8½-inch (14x21.5-cm) gift bag with handle (gold or other bright color)

Standard Supplies

- pencil
- ruler
- scissors
- stapler

Preparation

Trace Window Pattern onto front of bags, ¾ inch (1.9 cm) from bottom of bag. Cut out windows. Cut brown craft foam into one 5½x8½-inch (14x21.5-cm) rectangle for each child.

TREASURE TALK

Sometimes people put gifts in bags. What is the most special gift you have ever received? God gave us the most special gift ever when He sent His Son, Jesus. We don't have to wait until Christmas to thank God for giving us Jesus! God gave us Jesus because He loves us. God's love is giving!

Instruct each child in the following procedures:

- Use marker to write "God Gives Us Jesus" on bag above the window.
- Use foam shape stickers to design a nativity scene, including a star, manger, baby Jesus, etc. Use markers to draw faces on Joseph, Mary and baby Jesus.
- Peel backing off of stickers and press onto brown craft foam (sketch a).
- Slide foam scene into bag and staple to back of bag (sketch b).
- Use ribbon to tie bag handles together. With teacher's help, curl ends of ribbon.

Enrichment Idea

Create a bag to hold a gift by gluing nativity scene to inside front of bag, covering window opening. Place a sheet of tissue and your gift inside bag.

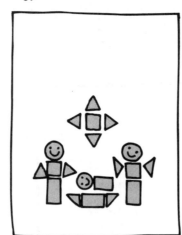

a.

b.

staples

God Gives Us Jesus

Window Pattern

Underwater Verse (30–40 MINUTES)

Materials

- poster board
- permanent wide-tip and fine-tip black markers
- food coloring in various colors
- ribbon

For each child—

- 8½x11-inch (21.5x28-cm) overhead transparency sheet

Standard Supplies

- scissors
- measuring stick
- copier paper
- glue
- shallow containers
- newspaper
- tape
- hole punch
- paintbrushes

Preparation

Cut poster board into four 10½x1-inch (26.5x2.5-cm) lengths and four 13x1-inch (33x2.5-cm) lengths for each child. With a marker, draw a 1-inch (2.5-cm) frame around edge of a sheet of copier paper and photocopy, making one paper for each child. Pour glue into shallow containers. Mix food coloring in glue to make several colors of glue paint. Cover work area with newspaper.

TREASURE TALK

I see that you are sharing the markers with each other. Thank you. Sharing is a way to be kind. What are some other ways we can be kind to friends? When you are kind, you are showing God's love because God's love IS kind!

Instruct each child in the following procedures:

- On paper and within frame, use markers to draw an underwater or beach scene. Use simple lines to outline items in picture. At bottom of paper, write "Love Is Kind."
- Tape transparency over top of sketch (sketch a).
- With wide-tip marker, trace all lines of sketch onto transparency. With fine-tip marker, trace over words of verse. Remove paper sketch.
- Glue four poster-board strips around the edges of picture to make a frame on one side of transparency.
- Turn picture over and glue remaining poster board strips to the back, aligning edges with front pieces (sketch b).
- Punch two holes in top of frame.
- With teacher's help, cut a 12-inch (30.5-cm) length of ribbon and thread through holes. Knot ends to make a hanger (sketch c).
- Turn transparency over to back side and paint inside sketch outlines with colored glue. Allow to dry.
- Hang your picture in a window for a stained-glass look.

Simplification Idea

Eliminate poster-board frame and punch holes directly in transparency for hanging.

Enrichment Idea

Place fish or island stickers (available from Gospel Light) onto bottom and sides of frame to decorate.

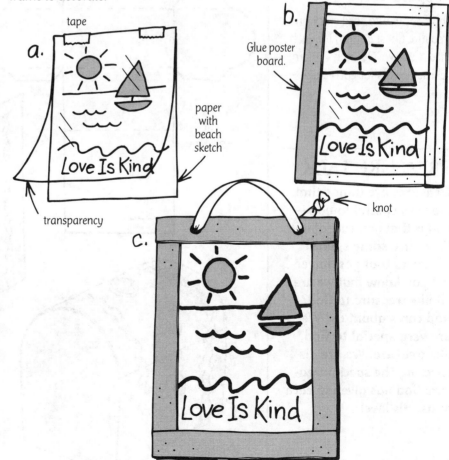

Precious Jewels Treasure Chest

(20–25 MINUTES)

Materials

- Treasure Chest Pattern
- brown card stock
- gold rickrack
- acrylic gems (available from Gospel Light)

For each child—

- ⅜-inch (.9-cm) round self-adhesive Velcro fastener
- several chocolate Kisses

Standard Supplies

- scissors
- ruler
- tape
- glue

Preparation

Photocopy onto card stock one Treasure Chest Pattern for each child. Cut two 7½-inch (19-cm) rickrack pieces for each child.

TREASURE TALK

Treasures are things that are very special to you— things that you care about. What are some special treasures that you have? Did you know that we are all like treasure to God? God cares about us! We are very special to God, like treasure! We are discovering the special treasure God has given to each of us: His love!

Instruct each child in the following procedures:

- Cut out Treasure Chest on solid lines (sketch a).
- With teacher's help, fold treasure chest on dashed lines and tape front, back and sides together (sketch b).
- Glue rickrack to chest about 1½ inches (4 cm) apart to make straps (sketch c).
- Attach the Velcro rounds together. Remove adhesive backing from both sides. Attach one side of Velcro to inside of front panel. Then press the other side onto the treasure chest front flap to close lid (sketch c).
- Glue jewels around outside of treasure chest (sketch d).
- Put several chocolate Kisses in your chest.
- After you eat your Kisses, you may store in your treasure chest "treasure" that you have received from SonTreasure Island.

Enrichment Idea

Photocopy Bible verses and cut apart into 2-inch (5-cm) strips. Children may roll up as scrolls and tie with ribbon. Children fill their chests with verses.

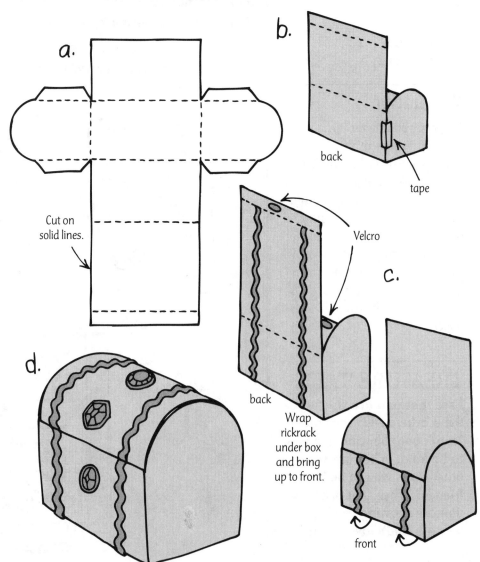

Treasure Chest Pattern

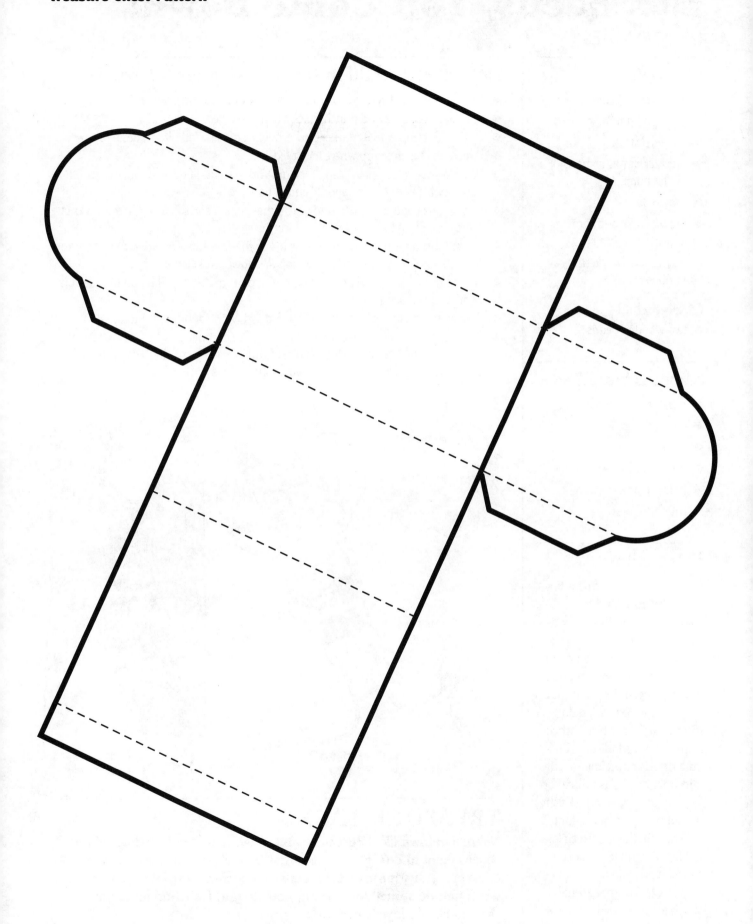

Younger Elementary • Grades 1-3   **65**

Zacchaeus, You Come Down!

(25–30 MINUTES)

Materials

- Zacchaeus Pattern
- Tree Top Pattern
- tan card stock
- green craft foam sheets or poster board
- brown yarn
- brown craft foam or construction paper
- permanent markers in various colors

For each child—
- two wooden beads

Standard Supplies

- scissors
- pen
- craft knife
- measuring stick
- hole punches
- masking tape

Preparation

Photocopy one Zacchaeus Pattern onto card stock for each child. Photocopy Tree Top Pattern onto card stock and cut out. Trace one Tree Top Pattern onto green craft foam or poster board for each child and cut out. Use pen to mark a dot where holes are to be punched in Tree Top (as indicated on pattern). Use craft knife to cut 3-inch (7.5-cm) slits in Tree Top for doorknob opening (sketch a). Cut yarn into one 4-foot (1.2-m) length for each child. Cut brown craft foam or construction paper into one 2x11-inch (5x28-cm) tree trunk shape for each child.

Instruct each child in the following procedures:

- Use markers to draw and color Zacchaeus's face, hair and clothes.
- Cut out Zacchaeus and punch holes where indicated.
- Outline Tree Top with a marker and draw tree details and birds if desired.
- Punch holes in Tree Top where indicated.
- Wrap a small piece of masking tape around one end of yarn to make sewing tip. Tie a double knot at the opposite end of yarn.
- Thread one bead onto yarn and pull to the knotted end of yarn. Make sure knot is big enough to hold the bead in place.
- Lay cutouts on table with Zacchaeus below the Tree Top. Thread yarn tip through the holes in Zacchaeus and in Tree Top as shown in sketch b.
- Thread the second bead onto the yarn. Cut off masking tape tip and tie a double knot to secure bead.
- Glue tree trunk to the back of the Tree Top, below the doorknob cutout.
- Place Tree Top opening over a doorknob. Slide Zacchaeus to the Tree Top. Alternately pull down on each side of yarn to watch Zacchaeus climb down (sketch c). Or gently pull yarn to the sides to watch Zacchaeus climb up.

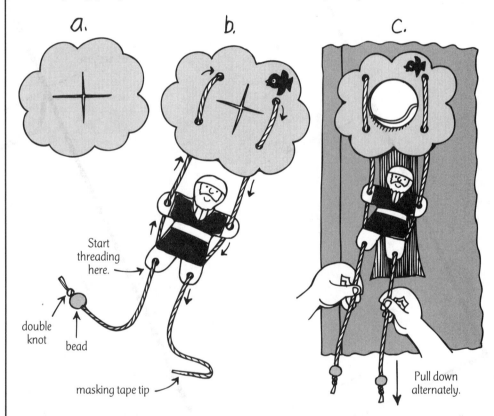

a.

b.

c.

Start threading here.

double knot

bead

masking tape tip

Pull down alternately.

TREASURE TALK

Nobody in town liked Zacchaeus. But after he met Jesus, what did Zacchaeus want to do? (He promised to give back all the money he took and even give more.) **Jesus forgave Zacchaeus. When someone loves you, even when you do something wrong, how do you feel? God loves you all the time. God's love is forgiving.**

**Tree Top and
Zaccheus
Patterns**

Tree Top Pattern

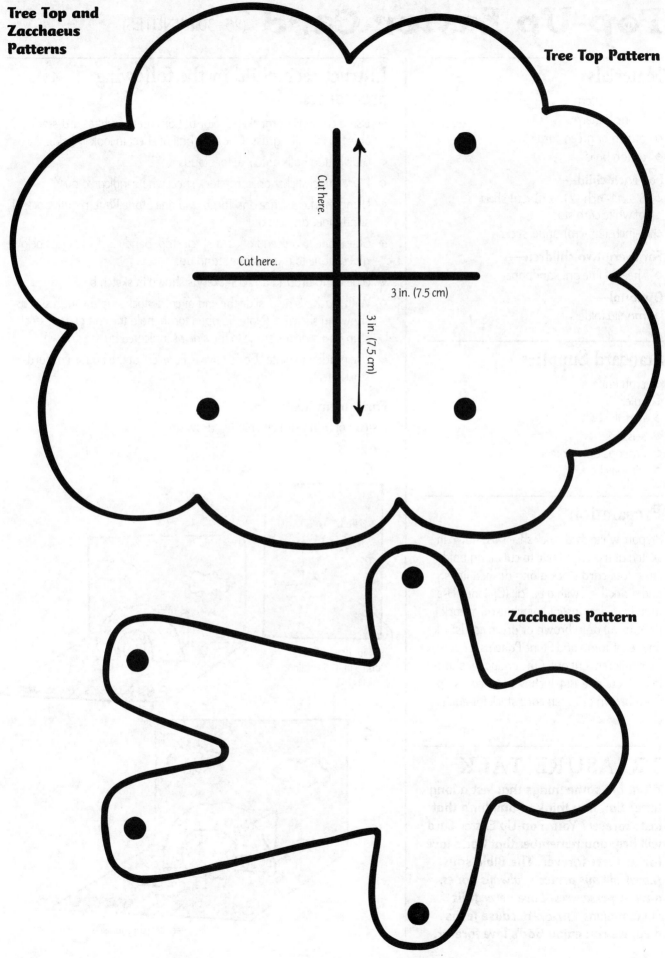

Cut here.

Cut here.

3 in. (7.5 cm)

3 in. (7.5 cm)

Zaccheus Pattern

Pop-Up Easter Card (25–30 MINUTES)

Materials
- ❖ Tomb Pattern
- ❖ Stone Pattern
- ❖ brown or green card stock
- ❖ cotton balls

For each child—
- ❖ 8½x11-inch (21.5x28-cm) sheet of white card stock
- ❖ 1-inch (2.5-cm) angel sticker

For every two children—
- ❖ sheet of fine grit sandpaper

Optional—
- ❖ manila folders

Standard Supplies
- ❖ craft knife
- ❖ ruler
- ❖ pencil
- ❖ scissors
- ❖ crayons or markers
- ❖ glue sticks

Preparation
Prepare white card-stock sheets as shown in sketch a; use craft knife to cut along bold lines, fold card stock along dashed lines, and mark the X with a pencil. (Optional: Use manila folders instead of white card stock.) Photocopy onto brown or green cardstock one set of Tomb and Stone Patterns for every four children. Cut out. Cut sandpaper sheets in half. Cut one 1x4-inch (2.5x10-cm) strip from brown or green card stock for each child.

TREASURE TALK
What are some things that last a long time? Can you think of anything that lasts forever? Your Pop-Up Easter Card will help you remember that God's love for us lasts forever. The Bible says, *[Love] always protects, always hopes, always perseveres. Love never fails* (1 Corinthians 13:7-8). **Because Jesus died, we can enjoy God's love forever.**

Instruct each child in the following procedures:
- ❖ Using crayons or markers, color bottom half of white card-stock sheet to look like grass. Color top half of sheet to look like sky.
- ❖ Glue cotton balls onto sky for clouds.
- ❖ Place angel sticker on card-stock sheet where indicated by X.
- ❖ Using markers, trace one Tomb and one Stone Pattern onto back of sandpaper and cut out.
- ❖ Glue stone to one end of card-stock strip. Bend card stock just below glued stone to make stone stand up.
- ❖ Glue tomb around angel sticker as shown in sketch b.
- ❖ With teacher's help, slide the end of card-stock strip through slits as shown in sketch c. (Note: To open tomb, hold the end of card stock strip and slide the stone to the side as indicated by the arrow.)
- ❖ Use marker to write "God's Love Is Forever" at the bottom of card-stock sheet.

Enrichment Idea
Instead of using sticker, children draw angel.

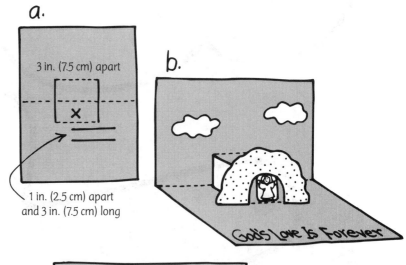

a.

3 in. (7.5 cm) apart

1 in. (2.5 cm) apart and 3 in. (7.5 cm) long

b.

God's Love Is Forever

c.

God's Love Is Forever

Insert tab through slits.

Stone and Tomb Patterns

Stone Pattern

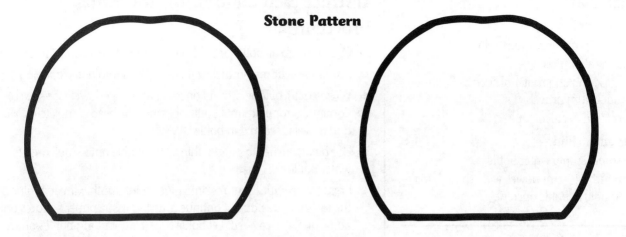

Tomb Pattern

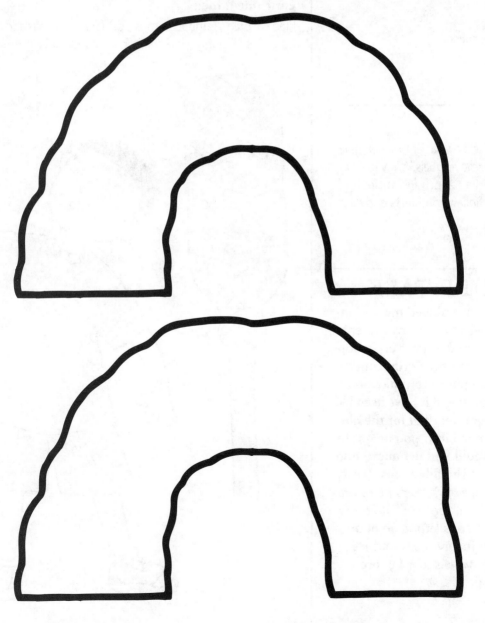

Island Maracas (20–25 MINUTES)

Materials

- blow-dryers
- tissue paper in various colors
- several funnels
- noise-making material such as beans or aquarium gravel
- colored electrical tape

For each child—
- small, empty water bottle
- 6-inch (15-cm) dowel, wide enough to fit snugly in bottle opening

Standard Supplies

- scissors
- glue
- shallow containers
- water
- paintbrushes

Preparation

Rinse bottles. Use blow-dryer to soften glue to more easily remove labels. Allow to dry. Cut tissue paper into 2-inch (5-cm) squares. Pour glue into shallow containers and dilute with water.

TREASURE TALK

Some of you have played musical instruments. What type of instruments have you played? Maracas are a popular instrument in the Caribbean. As you worked together to make your maracas, what would it have been like if every time you reached for the glue, someone bumped into you or got in your way? Would you get angry and hold a grudge? The Bible says, *[Love] is not easily angered, it keeps no record of wrongs* (1 Corinthians 13:5-6). Forgiving someone means letting go of our grudges. God forgives us, and He wants us to show His love by forgiving others, too.

Instruct each child in the following procedures:

- Use funnel to fill bottle one-third full with noise-making materials.
- Insert dowel approximately 2 inches (5 cm) into bottle opening.
- Wrap electrical tape around opening and over dowel (see sketch). Continue wrapping until bottle opening has been completely covered and dowel is secured to bottle.
- Use paintbrushes to paint a thin layer of glue onto small area of water bottle.
- Press tissue paper squares onto glue. Paint another layer of glue over the top of tissue paper. Continue pressing tissue paper squares onto bottle until it is covered. Let bottle dry. (Hint: Putting bottles on waxed paper or plastic wrap to dry will keep them from sticking to surfaces.)

Enrichment Idea

Play children's Caribbean music CD (*SonTreasure Island CD* available from Gospel Light) while children sing and shake maracas.

Younger Elementary • Grades 1-3

Section Three/Grades 4-6
Crafts for Older Elementary

Planning craft projects for older children can be fun. These children have well-developed skills to complete more-complicated projects and they love the chance to use those skills. However, preteens also have well-developed preferences about what they want to do. Sometimes a challenging project may not appeal to these young sophisticates, while a project that seems too juvenile to the adult will click with the kids!

We think you'll find projects in this section to satisfy the varied tastes of older elementary children. But a sense of humor and these tips will surely help: Filter craft ideas through a panel of experts—two or three fifth graders! If they like something, chances are the rest of the group will, too. Also, the better you get to know your children, the better your batting average will be. Remember, kids enjoy adapting crafts to express their own personalities—so put out a few extra supplies such as wiggle eyes, glitter glue, and fabric or paper scraps. You just might be surprised at what they dream up!

Oil Drum Painting (25–30 MINUTES)

Materials

- disposable foil cake pans (found at grocery stores)
- acrylic paints in various bright colors
- low-temperature glue gun
- black permanent wide-tip markers

For each child—

- large paper clip

Standard Supplies

- scissors
- ruler
- shallow containers
- narrow, round-tipped paintbrushes

Preparation

Flatten foil cake pans. Cut one 4-inch (10-cm) square for each child from pans. (Note: You will be able to get several from each pan.) Pour paint into shallow containers. Plug in glue gun out of reach of children.

Instruct each child in the following procedures:

- Use markers to outline bold designs or objects on foil square. Draw dots, curvy lines and stripes.
- Use acrylic paints to paint outlined designs.
- With teacher's help, use glue gun to glue paper clip to back of painting for a hanger.

Enrichment Ideas

Cut foil pans into different shapes (triangles, circles, rectangles, etc.). Children paint more than one picture. They attach pictures to hangers to make a mobile.

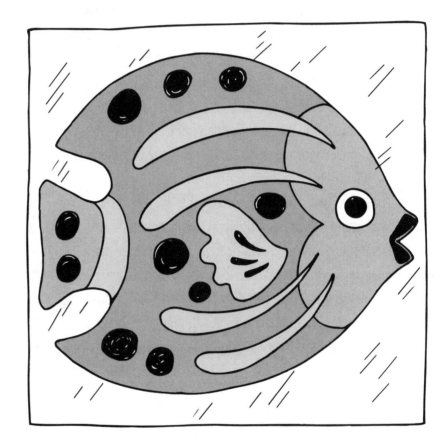

TREASURE TALK

On the island of Haiti, people use scraps of steel from large oil drums to create metal sculptures. They paint the sculptures with bright, bold-colored paints. These beautiful sculptures are used to decorate homes both inside and out.

Your painting can be a gift to someone you love. Who would you give your painting to? Giving and getting gifts is fun. How do you feel when you receive a gift? How about when you give one? Giving gifts is one way to show kindness to others. What are some other ways you can be kind? The Bible says, *Love is patient, love is kind. It does not envy, it does not boast, it is not proud* (1 Corinthians 13:4). When you are kind to others, you are showing God's love.

Forever Sand Castles (35–40 MINUTES)

Materials

- cardboard
- measuring cup
- sand
- cornstarch
- large saucepan
- mixing spoon
- stove or hot plate
- resealable plastic sandwich bags
- foil
- plastic knives
- toothpicks
- fine iridescent glitter
- spray bottles filled with water
- tiny seashells (available from craft stores)
- small twigs
- colored paper scraps

Standard Supplies

- craft knife
- ruler
- water
- shallow containers
- glue
- scissors

Preparation

Using craft knife, cut cardboard into one 8x6-inch (20.5x15-cm) rectangle for each child. Make one Sand Clay recipe for every three children: Measure 4 cups sand, 2 cups cornstarch and 3 cups water into saucepan. Mix well with spoon. Cook over medium heat until mixture thickens into a clay-like consistency. Remove from heat and allow to cool. Divide into three equal portions and place in sandwich bags. (Sand Clay may be made a day or two before modeling if kept in airtight containers or sealed plastic bags. Do not refrigerate.) Give one sandwich bag of clay to each child. Tear foil into one 10-inch (25.5-cm) length for each child. Set out shallow containers filled with water.

Instruct each child in the following procedures:

- Cover cardboard with foil. Working on foil-covered cardboard, take about one-third of Sand Clay and make a 5-inch (12.5-cm) round base to build your sand castle on.
- Use your finger to press a moat around the base (sketch a).
- Use remaining clay to build a small castle in center of base. Form a block shape for the main structure. Add cylinder shapes for towers and make cone shapes for roofs (sketch b). Apply water with fingers to help pieces adhere to each other.
- Use plastic knives and toothpicks to carve windows, doors or other details.
- While still damp, sprinkle castle with iridescent glitter. (If clay is no longer sticky, use spray bottle to mist sand castle with water first.)
- Decorate with small shells and twigs. To secure shells and twigs to sand castle, dot with glue and push into clay.
- Cut out and glue small colored paper flags to toothpicks. Then stick flags into clay on rooftops.
- Leave sand castle on foil-covered cardboard to air-dry for a few days or remove from cardboard and bake on foil piece in a 225°F oven for two hours. If parts of the castle come loose, simply reattach with glue. (Note: Remove toothpick flags before baking. Flags may be glued in holes after baking.)

Enrichment Idea

After sand castle has hardened, spray with clear acrylic spray.

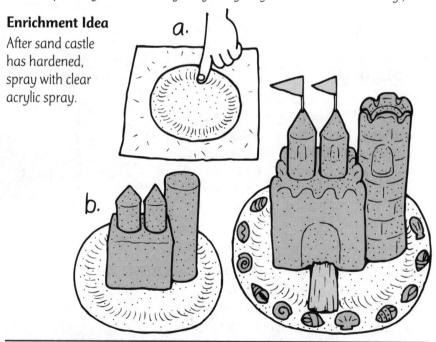

TREASURE TALK

Your sand castle will last a long time—much longer than a sand castle you would build on a beach. What other things can you think of that last a long, long time? Nothing here on Earth will last forever. But God's love for us is everlasting. He sent Jesus, His Son, to live, die and rise again so that we can live forever with Him. Your sand castle can remind you that when you believe in Jesus, God promises you eternal life and a place with Him, forever.

Materials

- ❖ Aquarium Fish Patterns
- ❖ Aquarium Coral Pattern
- ❖ craft foam in various bright colors
- ❖ low-temperature glue gun
- ❖ large and small paper clips
- ❖ blue food coloring
- ❖ glitter
- ❖ glycerin
- ❖ small shells (available from craft stores)
- ❖ plastic beads or aquarium gravel in various bright colors

For each child—

- ❖ pint-sized wide-mouth jelly jar with lid

Standard Supplies

- ❖ card stock
- ❖ scissors
- ❖ water
- ❖ plastic tubs
- ❖ pencils
- ❖ hole punch

Preparation

Photocopy onto card stock one set of Aquarium Fish and Coral Patterns for every three children. For each child, cut one craft-foam circle that is a little smaller than inside of jar lid. Fill plastic tubs with water. (Hint: If hard water is a problem in your area, use distilled water.) Plug in glue gun out of reach of children.

TREASURE TALK

What part of your aquarium do you "love"? What would you "love" to do if you could live underwater? Often we use the word "love" to describe something we want to do ("I'd LOVE to!") when we really mean that we would enjoy doing it—a lot! God created us to love people and to love Him. We can show how much we love people by the way we act toward them. It's easy to love someone who acts or thinks like you. How can you show love to people who are different from you?

Instruct each child in the following procedures:

- ❖ Cut out patterns.
- ❖ Use pencil to trace one of each pattern onto craft foam. Cut out foam shapes.
- ❖ Use hole punch to make eyes in fish.
- ❖ Bend paper clips as shown in sketch a. (Note: Using different sizes of paper clips will allow fish to "float" at different heights.)
- ❖ Hook paper clips through the bottom of fish bodies as shown in sketch b.
- ❖ Position fish on craft foam circle and push clips through foam to attach (sketch c).
- ❖ Ask teacher to use glue gun to put a puddle of glue inside center of jar lid. Push craft foam circle onto top of glue to secure (sketch c).
- ❖ Ask teacher to use glue gun to glue coral to craft-foam circle between fish.
- ❖ Dip jar in tub and fill to the top with water. To tint water, add one drop of blue food coloring.
- ❖ Add 1 teaspoon of glitter and two drops of glycerin to water in jar. (Note: Plastic glitter will float. Metal glitter will sink, causing a "snow globe" effect. Glycerin will help slow glitter down and keep it floating longer.) Add a small amount of shells and beads or gravel.
- ❖ Holding jar over tub, invert lid and screw onto jar so that aquarium scene is inside jar. Turn jar upside down so that lid is on the bottom and fish are floating upright (sketch d).

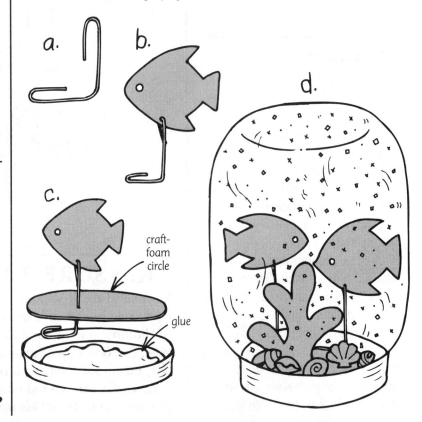

a.

b.

c.

d.

craft-foam circle

glue

Aquarium Fish and Aquarium Coral Patterns

Aquarium Fish Patterns

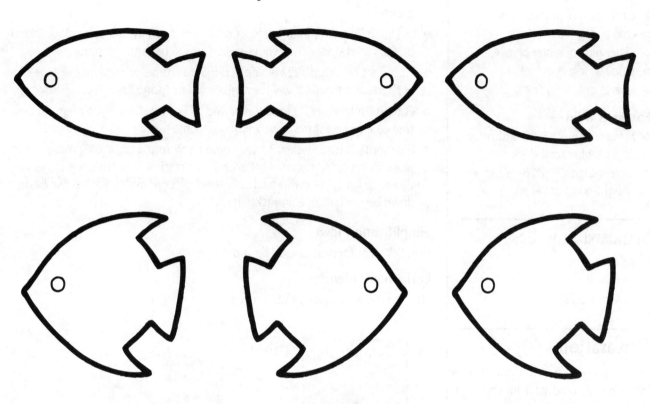

Aquarium Coral Pattern

Older Elementary • Grades 4-6

Underwater 3-D Picture (25–30 MINUTES)

Materials

- Underwater Patterns
- card stock in various colors
- colored fine-tip markers
- glitter glue or glitter pens
- small wiggle eyes
- thread or fishing line

For each child—

- 8½x11-inch (21.5x28-cm) sheet of dark-blue card stock
- 8½x11-inch (21.5x28-cm) sheet of light-blue card stock

Standard Supplies

- scissors
- glue or tape
- hole punches

Preparation

Photocopy one set of Underwater Patterns onto card stock for each child.

TREASURE TALK

There is a famous saying: "A picture paints a thousand words." Pictures oftentimes tell a story. If you could write a story to go with your 3-D picture, what kind of story would you write? (Adventure. Mystery. Nature. Science fiction.)

The Bible is the greatest book of all time. It has adventure, drama, mystery and history. But it's also a love story. The Bible tells us all about God's love for us. The Bible says, *This is how God showed his love among us: He sent his one and only Son into the world that we might live through him* (1 John 4:9). **God sent Jesus to show us His love.**

Instruct each child in the following procedures:

- Fold dark-blue card stock in half width-wise (sketch a). This will be the background.
- Cut out a large, irregular opening in the center of light-blue card stock (sketch b). Fold card stock in half width-wise. This will be the foreground.
- Place light-blue card stock on top of dark-blue card stock and glue or tape edges of short sides together with the center fold line facing toward you (sketch c).
- Cut out Underwater Patterns. Color and use glitter glue or glitter pens to decorate your sea creatures. Glue wiggle eyes onto fish.
- Glue some of Underwater Patterns onto background piece. Glue more Underwater Patterns to foreground. Punch holes in some fish. Cut small pieces of thread or fishing line, thread through holes in fish and tie so that fish hang down beyond the opening (sketch d).

Simplification Idea

Use stickers or foam shapes to decorate 3-D picture.

Enrichment Idea

Children use watercolor paints to decorate Underwater Patterns.

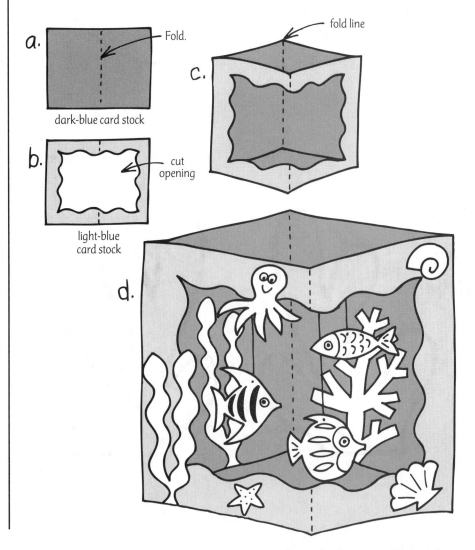

a. Fold. — dark-blue card stock

b. cut opening — light-blue card stock

c. fold line

d.

Underwater Patterns

Older Elementary • Grades 4-6

Starfish People (20–25 MINUTES)

Materials

- Starfish Clothing Patterns
- Starfish Figure Pattern
- low-temperature glue gun
- craft foam in various bright colors
- black permanent fine-tip markers

For each child—
- 2 large paperclips
- 2 suction cup hangers
- resealable sandwich bag

Standard Supplies

- card stock
- scissors
- pencils
- hole punches
- craft knife
- craft glue

Preparation

Photocopy onto card stock one set of Starfish Clothing Patterns for every four children. Photocopy one Starfish Figure onto card stock for each child. Plug in glue gun out of reach of children.

TREASURE TALK

Did you know that there are approximately 1,800 different species of starfish? Most species have five arms while others have as many as 50! Some live in deep water, while others live close to shore. God created all different kinds of starfish.

God created all different kinds of people, too. What do you think would happen if we all looked and acted the same? God uniquely created us because He cares about us and He wants us to care about others, even those who are different from us.

Instruct each child in the following procedures:

- Cut out Clothing Patterns.
- Trace two Starfish Figures onto craft foam and cut out.
- Trace clothing shapes onto foam and cut out. Use markers and craft foam scraps to add details to clothes and Starfish Figures. (Note: Use hole punch to make lens holes in sunglasses. Punch another color and insert punched hole shape into lens hole in glasses. Punched holes can also be used to decorate clothes.)
- Ask teacher to use craft knife to cut slits in sandals and hats.
- Glue clothes and accessories to Starfish Figures.
- With teacher's help, use glue gun to glue one end of paper clip to back of Starfish Figure's head as shown in sketch. Repeat for second Starfish Figure.
- Press suction cup to clean window or mirror. Hang Starfish Figure on suction cup hanger by paper clip. Store Starfish Figures and suction cups in resealable sandwich bag.

hot glue

Starfish Figure and Starfish Clothing Patterns

Starfish Clothing Patterns

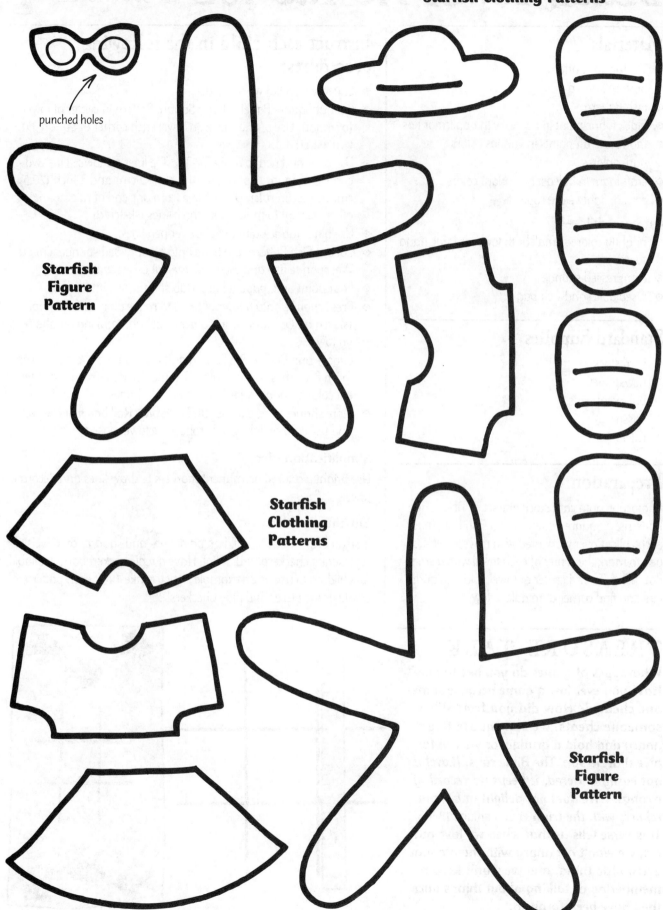

punched holes

Starfish Figure Pattern

Starfish Clothing Patterns

Starfish Figure Pattern

Materials

- Tic-Tac-Toe Patterns
- Square Pattern
- Fish Pattern
- black fabric paint in bottles with applicator tips
- fabric or craft paints in various colors
- paper plates
- craft foam in at least two bright colors
- cord or lightweight rope

For each child—

- brightly colored small bath towel or large hand towel
- compressed sponge
- resealable sandwich bag

Standard Supplies

- card stock
- newspaper
- ball point pens
- scissors
- rulers

Preparation

Photocopy onto card stock one set of Tic-Tac-Toe Patterns, a Square Pattern and a Fish Pattern for each child. Cover work area with newspaper. Use pen to mark the center of each towel with a small dot. (Hint: To find center of towel, fold into quarters and find corner at middle of towel.)

TREASURE TALK

What types of games do you like to play? Have you ever lost a game because someone cheated? How did you feel? When someone cheats, we can choose to get angry and hold a grudge, or we can forgive that person. The Bible says, *[Love] is not easily angered, it keeps no record of wrongs. Love does not delight in evil but rejoices with the truth* (1 Corinthians 13:5-6). This verse tells us that when we love others, we won't get angry with them about every little thing, and we won't keep remembering or talking about things once they have been forgiven.

Instruct each child in the following procedures:

- Lay towel on flat work surface.
- Cut out Square Pattern. Place Square Pattern in center of towel (over dot). Use pen to mark on towel each corner of Square Pattern with a dot.
- Use ruler and pen to make Tic-Tac-Toe lines on towel: Line two corners of square up with the 4-inch (10-cm) and 8-inch (20.5-cm) marks on ruler. Draw a line from one end of ruler to the other. Repeat to make other three lines (sketch a).
- Use black fabric paint to trace over pen lines.
- Cut out Fish Pattern and trace onto compressed sponge. Cut out. Wet sponge fish and then squeeze out excess water.
- Pour paint onto paper plates. Dab sponge fish into paint.
- Press sponge onto border of towel to make painted fish shape (sketch b). Continue, using other colors and making a pattern on towel.
- Choose one Tic-Tac-Toe Pattern and trace onto one color of craft foam five times. Trace another Tic-Tac-Toe Pattern onto a different color of foam five times. Cut out all shapes.
- Store shapes in resealable sandwich bag. Roll bag inside towel and use cord or lightweight rope to tie towel closed.

Simplification Idea

Use brightly colored permanent markers to draw lines and decorate towels.

Enrichment Idea

Instead of Tic-Tac-Toe, children paint lines and squares on towels to represent a checkerboard. (Hint: Have a real checkerboard available for children to use as an example.) They make 12 of each pattern to create game pieces and play Checkers!

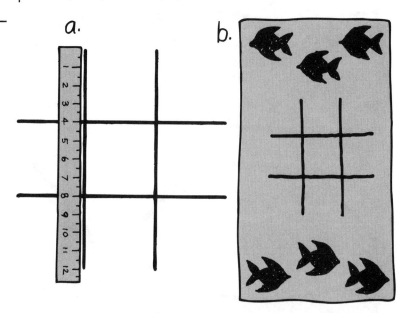

a.   b.

Square, Fish and Tic-Tac-Toe Patterns

Square Pattern

Fish Pattern

Tic-Tac-Toe Patterns

Kaleidoscope of Kindness

(25–30 MINUTES)

Materials

- silver metallic card stock
- corrugated cardboard
- several overhead transparencies
- low-temperature glue gun
- yellow electrical tape
- plastic bubble wrap
- various kaleidoscope fillers (small seashells, beads, sea glass, sequins, gem stones, plastic confetti, aquarium gravel, etc.)

For each child—

- 2 potato chip can lids
- clean potato chip can

Standard Supplies

- scissors
- ruler
- glue
- craft knife
- transparent tape

Preparation

Cut silver card stock in half widthwise so that there is one half for each child. With a ruler and the sharp edge of scissors, score a line 2 inches (5 cm) from each 8½-inch (21.5-cm) edge of each card stock half (sketch a). Cut cardboard into one 8½ x ¾-inch (21.5x1.9-cm) strip for each child. Cut transparencies to make two 3-inch (7.5-cm) squares for each child. Using only half of the lids and with craft knife, cut dime-sized holes in the center of lids to make one lens for each child. Remove the bottom end from each potato chip can. Plug in glue gun out of reach of children.

Instruct each child in the following procedures:

- Wrap electrical tape around the outside of potato chip can. This is the case of the kaleidoscope.
- Trim one of the transparency squares to fit inside the lid over the lens hole. Tape in place (sketch b).
- Glue lens lid to one end of can.
- Fold card stock along scored lines to form a triangular tube. The silver side should be on the inside of the tube. Tape the edges together along entire length to form "mirror" tube (sketch c).
- Wrap the "mirror" tube with bubble wrap and use transparent tape to secure. Slide the tube into the kaleidoscope to meet the lens. The bubble wrap keeps the tube from shifting.
- Bend the corrugated strip into a circle and fit inside the end of the kaleidoscope. If needed, cut the corrugated strip so that the ends meet without overlapping. Remove the strip from the kaleidoscope and tape the ends together.
- With teacher's help, use glue gun to glue the corrugated circle to the second transparency square. Trim transparency edges even with circle (sketch d).
- Place corrugated circle piece in the end of kaleidoscope with the transparency against end of the "mirror" tube.
- Partially fill end section with assorted kaleidoscope filler materials (sketch e) so that filler can move around when kaleidoscope is turned.
- Glue the second lid on top to seal kaleidoscope.

Enrichment Idea

Instead of using electrical tape, children decorate plain paper with island designs, using paint, stencils, stamps, stickers, crayons, felt pens, etc., and wrap around outside of potato chip can.

TREASURE TALK

You demonstrated a lot of patience as you made your kaleidoscope. What are the results of having patience? (The craft is completed. We have something fun to take home.) **When are times you've needed patience? What was the result of having patience in that situation? What would have happened if you didn't have patience? God wants us to have patience with people, too. We show love to others when we're patient with them.**

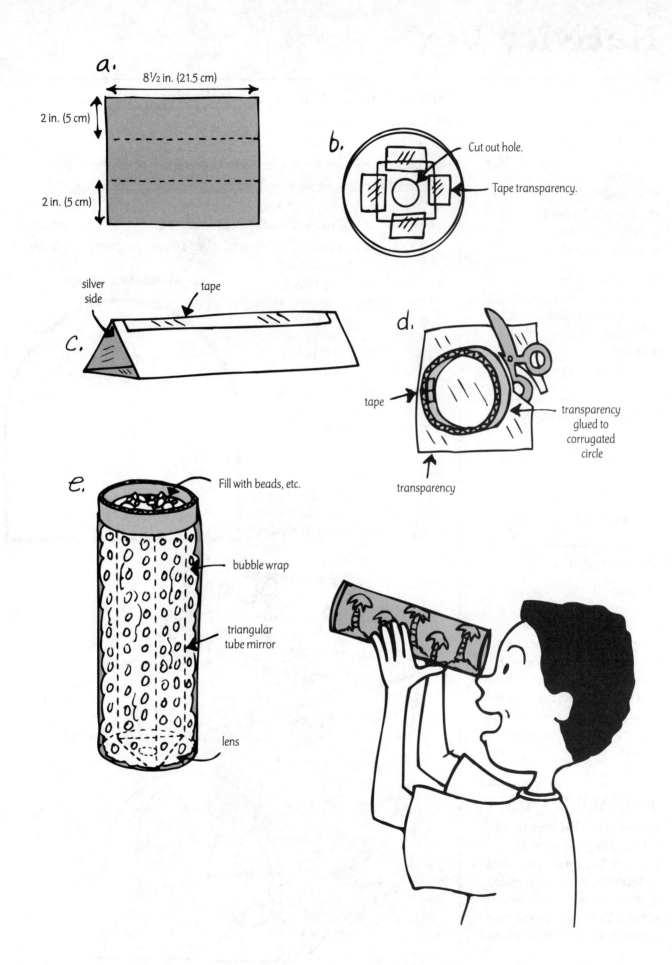

a.

8½ in. (21.5 cm)

2 in. (5 cm)

2 in. (5 cm)

b.

Cut out hole.

Tape transparency.

c.

silver side

tape

d.

tape

transparency glued to corrugated circle

transparency

e.

Fill with beads, etc.

bubble wrap

triangular tube mirror

lens

Nativity Box (25–30 MINUTES)

Materials

- Window Pattern
- low-temperature glue gun
- self-hardening clay in various colors
- toothpicks
- permanent marker
- brown craft foam
- curling ribbon

For each child—

- one pint-sized take-out container (available at restaurant supply stores)
- angel sticker
- small die-cut star

Standard Supplies

- card stock
- pencils
- scissors
- ruler
- hole punch

Preparation

Photocopy one Window Pattern onto card stock. Trace pattern onto one side of each food container. Cut out. Measure around bottom of container and cut a piece of card stock slightly smaller to fit inside bottom; cut enough to make one bottom piece for every four children. Plug in glue gun out of reach of children.

TREASURE TALK

God showed His love to us by sending His own Son, Jesus, to live among us. And because God loves us, every day we can show His love to others. When are some times you can show love to others?

Instruct each child in the following procedures:

- Use clay to form Mary, Joseph and baby Jesus figures.
- Use toothpicks to draw facial features in clay.
- Use permanent marker to write "God Gave Us Jesus" above the window.
- Trace shape of container bottom onto brown craft foam and cut out.
- With teacher's help, use glue gun to glue Mary onto craft foam rectangle, holding Mary in place until glue sets. Repeat gluing process to add Joseph to scene.
- With teacher's help, use glue gun to glue baby Jesus figure in front of Mary and Joseph. Let cool.
- Use angel sticker and die-cut star to decorate outside of container. Place angel sticker near window. Punch hole in star and use small piece of ribbon to hang from metal handle.
- Cut a 3-foot (.9-m) length of curling ribbon. Tie ribbon to container handle and use scissors to curl ends.

Enrichment Idea

Use clay to form animals to place in stable. Add small bits of hay to sprinkle on floor of manger scene.

Window Pattern

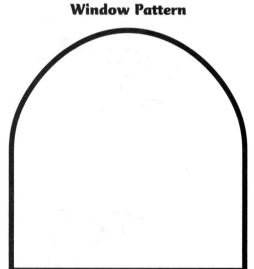

Love Is Patient Bulletin Board

(25–30 MINUTES)

Materials

- Fish Pattern
- waxed paper
- small cardboard rectangles or paintbrushes
- craft foam in various bright colors
- craft cement
- small seashells (available from craft stores)
- thumbtacks
- fabric paints in various bright colors

For each child—

- 11x14-inch (28x35.5-cm) piece of foam board
- 15x18-inch (38x45.5-cm) piece of ocean- or tropical-print cotton fabric
- two 7-inch (18-cm) rubber bands in various colors

Optional—

- precut craft foam fish shapes (available at craft stores)

Standard Supplies

- scissors
- measuring stick
- card stock
- craft glue
- pencils

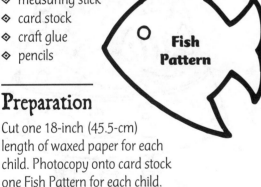

Fish Pattern

Preparation

Cut one 18-inch (45.5-cm) length of waxed paper for each child. Photocopy onto card stock one Fish Pattern for each child.

TREASURE TALK

A bulletin board is a good place to put things that you don't want to forget about. What will you hang on your bulletin board? Writing your Bible verse at the top will help you remember what the Bible says about being patient and kind. When are some times it is hard to be patient? Kind? When we are patient and kind, God's love will be obvious to others.

Instruct each child in the following procedures:

- Squeeze craft glue around one side of foam board.
- Use cardboard rectangles or paintbrushes to evenly spread glue over entire surface of foam board.
- Lay fabric, print-side down, on waxed paper.
- Lay foam board, glue-side down, in center of back side of fabric.
- Squeeze a line of glue around edge of uncovered side of foam board. Wrap edge of fabric over glue and press in place (sketch a). Let dry.
- Cut out Fish Pattern. Trace fish shapes onto craft foam and cut out. Use craft cement to glue foam fish shapes and small shells to heads of thumbtacks. Let dry. (Optional: Use precut craft foam fish shapes.)
- Use fabric paints to write "Love Is Patient" at top of board.
- Wrap ends of large rubber band over opposite corners of board. Repeat with second rubber band on remaining corners (sketch b).

Simplification Idea

Use colored permanent markers to write words at top of bulletin board.

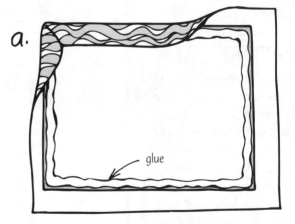

a.

glue

b.

Love Is Patient

Ocean Wind Chime (25–30 MINUTES)

Materials

- craft paint in various colors
- paper plates
- cotton string or twine

For each child—

- 5-inch (12.5-cm) diameter terra-cotta pot
- 3-inch (7.5-cm) dowel
- three 7-inch (18-cm) dowels

Standard Supplies

- newspaper
- paintbrushes
- scissors
- measuring stick
- glue

Preparation

Pour paint onto paper plates. Cover work area with newspaper.

TREASURE TALK

What makes chimes move? (Wind.) **In some ways, God is like the wind. We can't see Him, but we know He is always with us. God cares about us. Who are some people you care about? It's easy to show love and care to people we love—like our friends and families—but God's love is for EVERYONE—even people others don't care about.**

Instruct each child in the following procedures:

- Use paintbrushes to paint an ocean or beach scene on outside of pot. Let dry.
- Knot the center of one piece of string around the center of 3-inch (7.5-cm) dowel and then knot ends of string together to make hanger (sketch a).
- Knot one piece of string 1 inch (2.5 cm) from end of one 7-inch (18-cm) dowel. Wrap string four times around stick and knot again (sketch b). Repeat with remaining dowels.
- Tie strings on the 7-inch (18-cm) dowels to the 3-inch (7.5-cm) dowel so that dowels hang down about 2 inches (5 cm) as shown in sketch c. Trim ends of string.
- Coat each knot with glue.
- Thread knot at end of hanger through hole of inverted pot (sketch d). Hang chime and let glue on knots dry.

Enrichment Idea

Use glitter or gel marker to write "God's Love Is Caring" around the base of the pot.

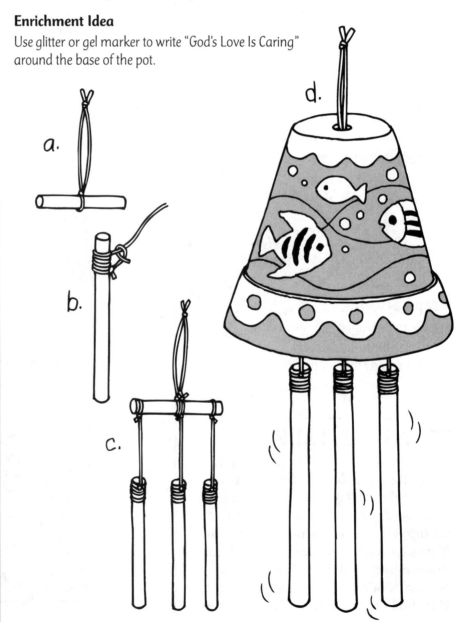

Island Scrapbook (30–45 MINUTES)

Materials

- cardboard
- sandpaper
- felt
- drill
- ¼-inch (.6-cm) drill bit
- wooden plank
- craft foam

For each child—

- 3 loose-leaf metal rings (available at office supply stores)
- several sheets of three-hole-punched white paper

Standard Supplies

- scissors
- measuring stick
- glue
- pencil

Preparation

Cut two 9x12-inch (23x30.5-cm) cardboard rectangles for each child. Cut one 12x19-inch (30.5x48.5-cm) sandpaper rectangle for each child. Cut one 12x19-inch (30.5x48.5-cm) felt rectangle for each child. Save felt scraps. Set up drill on wood plank out of reach of children. (Note: You will need careful adult supervision when helping children work with drill.)

TREASURE TALK

Scrapbooks can help us remember people and places that we love. Do you think you could keep your scrapbook forever? What might happen to it? Can you think of anything that lasts forever? There is one thing that lasts forever. God wants us to know that His love for us never stops. The Bible says, *[Love] always protects, always trusts, always hopes, always perseveres. Love never fails* (1 Corinthians 13:7-8). **God wants us to know that even though other things may not last, His love will never fail!**

Instruct each child in the following procedures:

- Line up edges of cardboard pieces on sandpaper piece, leaving a 1-inch (2.5-cm) gap in the center (sketch a).
- Glue large felt piece onto cardboard pieces.
- Fold book in half and mark three evenly spaced holes as shown in sketch b. (Hint: You can use a piece of three-hole-punched notebook paper as a guide.) With teacher's help, drill holes through cardboard, felt and sandpaper.
- Attach metal rings through holes.
- Cut craft foam into letters and shapes. Glue onto sandpaper to decorate scrapbook with an island scene (sketch c).
- Add paper to your scrapbook.

Simplification Idea

Instead of using sandpaper, cover both sides of cardboard with felt or cover cardboard with self-adhesive paper.

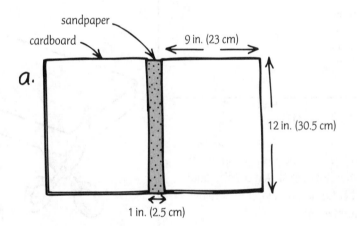

sandpaper
cardboard
9 in. (23 cm)
a.
12 in. (30.5 cm)
1 in. (2.5 cm)

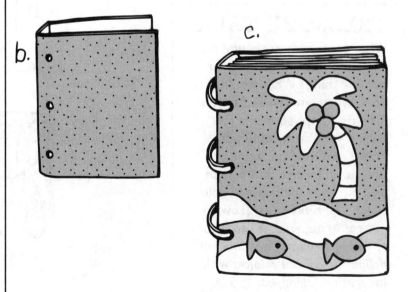

b.

c.

Chest O' Treasure (20–25 MINUTES)

Materials

- brown paper bags
- shoe box with lid
- low-temperature glue gun
- acrylic gems (available from Gospel Light)
- elastic
- treasure items (bead necklaces, bracelets and rings, ring pops, chocolate coins, candy necklaces, shells, fake gems, stickers, etc.)

Optional—

- hole punch
- paper fasteners

Standard Supplies

- scissors
- ruler
- glue
- water
- shallow containers

Preparation

Cut brown paper bags to make 4-inch (10-cm) squares. Cut shoe-box lids as shown in sketch a. Mix equal parts of glue and water in shallow containers.

TREASURE TALK

What are the treasures you put in your chest? Which is your favorite thing? What would you do if, when you reached for the last (ring pop) someone else took it first? You could get angry and hold a grudge or you could forgive that person and put something else in your chest. The Bible says, *[Love] is not easily angered, it keeps no record of wrongs. Love does not delight in evil but rejoices with the truth* (1 Corinthians 13:5-6).

Instruct each child in the following procedures:

- With teacher's help, use glue gun to squeeze a thick line of glue onto inside cut edge of lid. Attach lid to box by lining up back of box and glued edge of lid and pressing together (sketch b). (Optional: For added security and before gluing, punch three holes in back of box and cut edge of lid and line up so holes match. After adding glue but before glue dries, quickly place paper fasteners through holes in lid and box. Press lid to box.)
- Crumple and smooth out brown-bag squares.
- Dip brown-bag squares into glue and water mixture and glue to outside of shoe box and lid. Cover box and lid with overlapping squares making sure to wrap over all edges (sketch c).
- Glue gems onto chest to decorate.
- With teacher's help, use glue gun to glue one large jewel on center front of chest. Punch hole in front of lid as shown in sketch c. Measure elastic to loop snugly over jewel and then thread ends of elastic through hole in lid. Knot securely and use glue gun to glue knot to inside of lid. To close chest, pull elastic over jewel.
- Fill your chest with treasures.

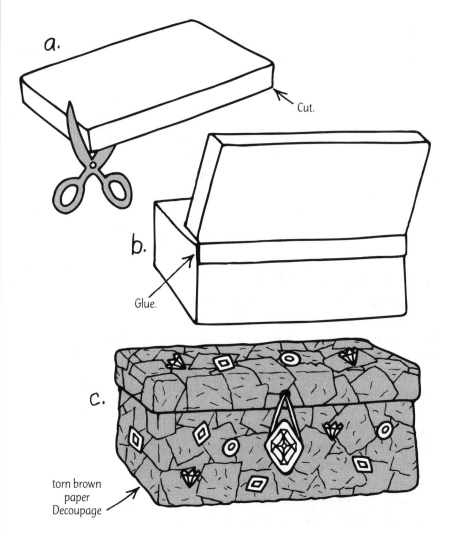

a.

Cut.

b.

Glue.

c.

torn brown paper Decoupage

Sandpaper Stationery (15–20 MINUTES)

Materials

- ❖ fine sandpaper
- ❖ ironing boards
- ❖ white copier paper
- ❖ irons

Standard Supplies

- ❖ scissors
- ❖ ruler
- ❖ newspaper
- ❖ crayons

Preparation

Cut sandpaper to make several 2x5-inch (5x12.5-cm) rectangles for each child. Cover ironing board with newspaper.

TREASURE TALK

The Bible says, [Love] is not rude, it is not self-seeking (1 Corinthians 13:5). **Someone who is not self-seeking thinks about others and takes time to show God's love. You can use your stationery to send a letter to someone you love. Who will you write to on your Sandpaper Stationery?**

Instruct each child in the following procedures:

- ❖ Use crayons to draw a beach or ocean design on sandpaper (sketch a). If desired, color additional designs on other sheets of sandpaper.
- ❖ Place white paper on ironing board. Place colored sandpaper facedown on top edge of paper (sketch b). With teacher's help, iron until design is transferred to paper.
- ❖ Make additional sheets of stationery by applying more color to original design or using a new design and ironing onto another sheet of paper.

Enrichment Ideas

Children create complementary designs to decorate envelopes. Children place stationery and envelopes together and tie with ribbon or raffia.

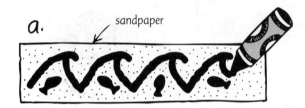

a.   sandpaper

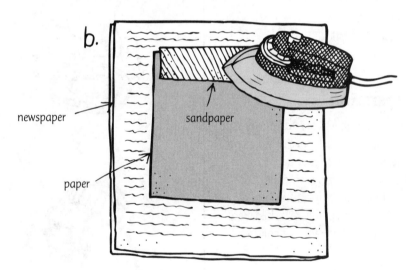

b.

newspaper

sandpaper

paper

Dear Grandma,

I Want to See Jesus Maze (25–30 MINUTES)

Materials

- Maze Master
- Jesus Pattern
- Zacchaeus Pattern
- green copier paper
- tan card stock
- low-temperature glue gun
- double-stick tape

For each child—

- ¾-1 inch (1.9-2.5 cm) diameter steel washer
- ¾-inch (1.9-cm) extra-strong button magnet
- craft stick

For every two children—

- 22x28-inch (56x71-cm) sheet of poster board

Standard Supplies

- scissors
- measuring stick
- markers

Preparation

Photocopy one Maze Master onto green paper for each child. Photocopy one Jesus and one Zacchaeus Pattern onto card stock for each child. Cut poster board into one 11x14-inch (28x35.5-cm) piece for each child. Plug in glue gun out of reach of children.

TREASURE TALK

Zacchaeus made a lot of people angry when he took their money. Has someone ever cheated you? How did that make you feel? It's not always easy to get along with our friends and the people in our families. Being kind to people who have been unkind to us is a way we can show forgiveness. Forgiveness is an important part of showing God's love.

Instruct each child in the following procedures:

- Use double-stick tape to attach maze to center of poster board.
- Color and cut out Jesus and Zacchaeus figures.
- Use double-stick tape to attach Jesus figure by the word "Finish" on the maze (do not cover any of the maze).
- Fold tabs on Zacchaeus figure as shown in sketch. With teacher's help, use glue gun to glue tabs to washer (see sketch).
- With teacher's help, use glue gun to glue magnet to end of craft stick—magnetic side up.
- To use: Hold maze in one hand. Place Zacchaeus figure at "Start." Hold magnet on stick underneath maze. Use magnet to guide Zacchaeus through the maze to Jesus.

hot glue

Zacchaeus Pattern

Jesus Pattern

Maze Master

Start

Finish

The Greatest Treasure Candle

(TWO-DAY CRAFT/40–50 MINUTES TOTAL TIME)

Materials

- The Greatest Treasure Pattern
- two large coffee cans
- hammer and nail
- candle wicking (found at craft supply stores)
- saucepan
- hot plate or stove
- oven mitt
- blue and green crayons
- paint stirring stick
- ice
- large shallow tubs or baking pans
- fine-tip markers in various colors
- blue netting
- twine or rope
- small rubber bands

For each child—

- large frozen juice can
- ½ lb. paraffin wax
- pencil
- 4 to 6 small trinkets for treasures (small shells, heart or cross brass charms, jewel-like beads, small polished rocks, etc.)

Standard Supplies

- scissors
- ruler
- water
- masking tape

DAY ONE Preparation

Photocopy one The Greatest Treasure Pattern for each child. Squeeze the openings of coffee cans together to form spouts (sketch a). With hammer and nail, poke a hole in the bottom of each juice can. For each child, cut a piece of candle wicking 2 inches (5 cm) longer than the height of juice can. Approximately 10 minutes before melted wax will be used, heat water in saucepan to boiling. Set one coffee can in saucepan and place half of the paraffin in the can. Melt one pound of wax for every four children. Add six to eight green crayons for every one pound of wax. With paint stirring stick, blend color into wax. This is for the first layer of candle. Place ice in tubs or baking pans. Note: When children begin to pour their first layer, begin melting wax in the other coffee can for second layer. Use one pound of wax and six to eight blue crayons for every four children.

Instruct each child in the following procedures:

- Poke candle wick through hole in the bottom of juice can. Tie a knot in the wick at bottom of juice can to block the hole.
- Use masking tape to cover the knotted wick and seal the hole on the bottom of the can (sketch b).
- Set pencil on top of can. Tape the unknotted end of the wick to a pencil to hold the wick upright (sketch c).
- Place can firmly on bottom of pan of ice. Pack ice around it.
- Place two or three small trinkets in the bottom of the can.
- Have teacher pour a 1-inch (2.5-cm) layer of green wax into juice can. Allow to set until wax is hard enough to place additional trinkets on top (about 15 minutes).
- While wax is setting, use markers to color "The Greatest Treasure." Cut out.
- Once wax is set, lay two or three trinkets in juice can on top layer of green wax.
- Have teacher pour a layer of blue wax into can until it is half full (sketch c). Allow candle to cool in pan of ice until hardened. (Teacher may remove candles from pan later in the day.)

DAY TWO Preparation

Cut one 12-inch (30.5-cm) square of blue netting for each child. Cut one 12-inch (30.5-cm) length of rope or twine for each child.

Instruct each child in the following procedures:

- Remove tape from bottom of juice can.
- Use scissors to cut off knot at bottom of can.
- Cut cardboard sides of can and tear away cardboard to reveal candle (sketch d).
- Trim wick to ½ inch (1.3 cm) in length.
- Set candle in center of netting square. Gather all sides of netting around candle and secure at the top with a rubber band.
- Tie length of twine or rope around rubber band and secure with a knot.
- Roll up "The Greatest Treasure" paper into a scroll. Then tie twine over the scroll and make a bow (sketch e).
- Give your treasure candle as a gift to someone with whom you'd like to share God's love. As the candle burns, the treasures will appear! (Note: Treasure trinkets should be removed carefully with tweezers from the hot wax after candle has been extinguished.)

Enrichment Idea

Pour a thin layer of sand in the bottom of can before adding wax. Brush off excess before wrapping in netting.

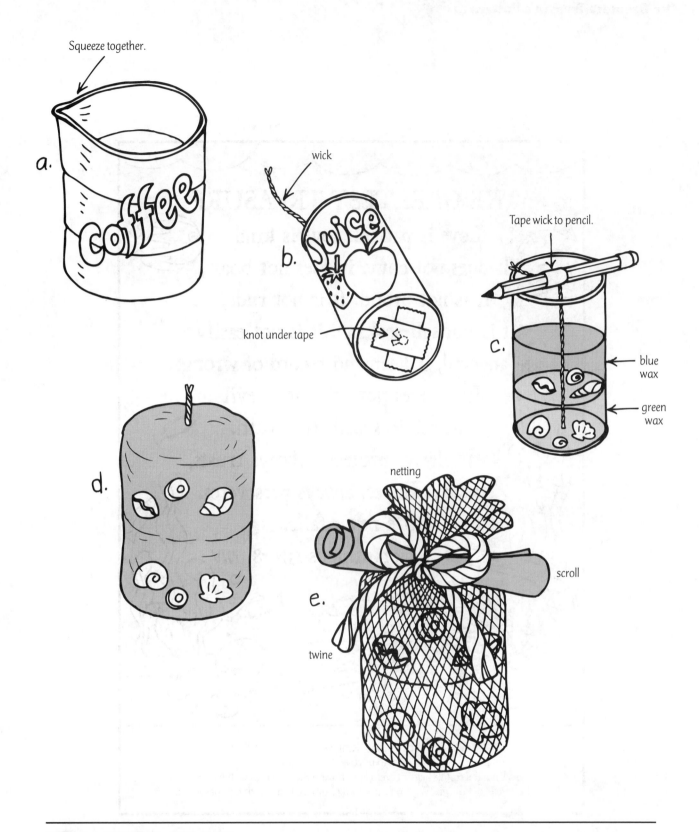

Squeeze together.

a.

Coffee

wick

b.

Juice

knot under tape

Tape wick to pencil.

c.

blue wax

green wax

d.

netting

scroll

e.

twine

TREASURE TALK

What would you like to find in a treasure chest? What would you do with your treasure? Having nice things is fine, but God's love is the greatest treasure of all. The Bible tells us that God loves us all the time. His love never gets lost, wears out, breaks, runs out of batteries or gets old and out-dated. God's love is the greatest treasure because it lasts forever!

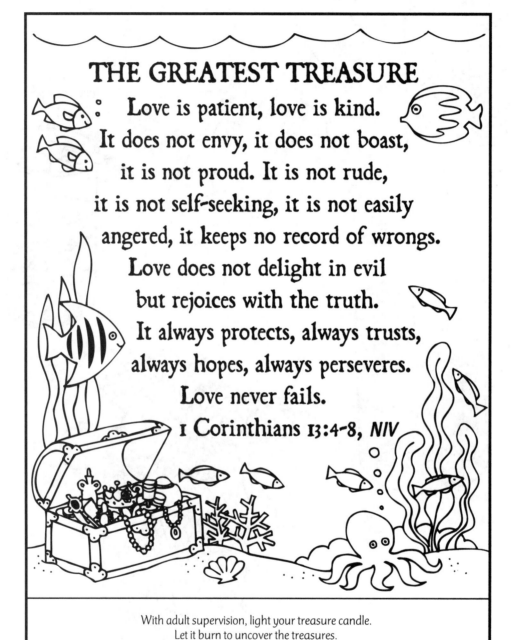

THE GREATEST TREASURE

Love is patient, love is kind. It does not envy, it does not boast, it is not proud. It is not rude, it is not self-seeking, it is not easily angered, it keeps no record of wrongs. Love does not delight in evil but rejoices with the truth. It always protects, always trusts, always hopes, always perseveres. Love never fails.

1 Corinthians 13:4-8, *NIV*

With adult supervision, light your treasure candle.
Let it burn to uncover the treasures.
Blow out the candle before carefully removing the treasures with tweezers.
Be careful of hot wax. Wipe off excess wax from treasures with a paper towel.

Index of Crafts